STORIES FROM THE HEART OF IRELAND

Brendan Power was born in Fethard on Sea in Co Wexford and in the 1950s became part of the Irish diaspora, moving to the UK with his family. After leaving school, he worked for the *Daily Express* before joining Radio 270, a pirate station anchored in the middle of the North Sea. When the government closed down the pirate stations he was offered a position with Radio Antilles in Montserrat, the Emerald Isle of the Caribbean, where he spent five years. Upon returning to England, he was involved in the launch of BRMB Radio in Birmingham, one of the new commercial stations in the UK. He is a founder and past president of the Professional Speaking Association and for many years was seen as one of Europe's leading motivational speakers, making him popular with major companies and organisations on four continents. He has written for numerous newspapers and magazines, is a former correspondent for the Associated Press, and is the author of two books, *Power Selling* and *Heroes of the Helen Blake*. In 2012 he completed the circle by returning to Fethard on Sea where he now lives in blissful, and active, retirement.

STORIES FROM THE HEART OF IRELAND

COMPILED BY BRENDAN POWER

Proceeds from the sale of this book will go to Make-A-Wish Ireland

Published by
Red Stripe Press
an imprint of
Orpen Press
Upper Floor, Unit B3
Hume Centre
Hume Avenue
Park West Industrial Estate
Dublin 12
Ireland

email: info@orpenpress.com
www.orpenpress.com

Paperback ISBN 978-1-78605-200-1
ePub ISBN 978-1-78605-201-8

Printed in the EU.

For
Sebastian, Niamh & Rosie

and all those children who will
see their dreams become reality

Acknowledgements

Each one of our authors has donated their story, their time and their talent, and it is thanks to their generosity that we have been able to produce this book. You will find their details at the back of the book. There are 61 stories, which I'm sure will provide you with a great deal of pleasure, but even more importantly – in buying this book you are also *giving* a great deal of pleasure by helping to make a child's wish become reality. The most inspirational story of all is not *in* the book; it is the reason for the book. Make-A-Wish Ireland is a remarkable organisation, making wishes come true for children with life-threatening conditions. The care and compassion of the staff is humbling, whilst the strength and resilience of the children is both heart-warming and heart-rending, and alongside these are the unsung heroes, the parents. Their hearts are broken, they are enduring every parent's worst nightmare, yet they still manage to maintain their dignity and provide never-ending support for their loved ones. I only wish we could all have their strength and their courage.

Thanks too …

Without the help of others, this book would never have come to fruition so I owe a great deal of thanks to Tom Nunan who originally suggested the idea and then went on to support it in many ways behind the scenes, to Garrett Bridgman and Lyndsey Collier of An Post who kindly provided stamps for the not inconsiderable number of letters sent to people throughout the country, to rail historian Jonathan Beaumont for sharing his knowledge, to Phillip Khan-Panni and Fiona McGinty for their expertise in editing, to Kathryn Thomas for her help in getting stories, to Michael Brennan for his belief in the project and to Paul Feldstein for his invaluable advice.

Contents

Contents

Contents

Contents

Contents

THE GIRL WITH SIXTY-FIVE ROSES

Eimear Ní Bhraonáin

Once upon a time, there was a beautiful little girl who inspired me with her remarkable bravery.

Her name was Gillian Dempsey. By the time I met her, it was 2008, and she had already endured more hardship than most of us could imagine in a lifetime. Yet Gillian was only in Third Class. She was waiting for a double lung transplant and had been in and out of Crumlin hospital since the day she was born.

When Gillian was diagnosed with Cystic Fibrosis, she was so young, she couldn't pronounce it. As a two-year-old, she told people she had 'Sixty-five roses'.

I've had the privilege of hearing so many stories day in, day out, meeting hundreds of people every year. I've been in homes, at the scenes of horrific tragedies, sat in courthouses, and listened to people revealing disturbing truths, and at times sharing joyous occasions, lifting cups and celebrating success.

There are so many names, so many families, so many faces. The time we spend together can be very intense, but very short. I try to remember people's names, details and faces. I've been working for more than two decades in news, so my memory is not as good as it used to be.

Sometimes, I meet people who say, 'Remember you interviewed me about the floods in Athlone?' or 'Remember the time my granny's house went on fire?' I always rack my brain trying to remember which flood, which fire, and sometimes I do, but the news cycle is so relentless.

Meeting a journalist and sharing your story is a huge event in somebody's life, and I've always felt fortunate to be the one entrusted by a person or family to give them a platform. I don't take it for granted and I believe in the power of storytelling. We help others by shining the light in the dark corners.

Your survival in news often relies on having a tough exterior. You need endurance skills for the long coroners' court sittings, a stomach for horrific crimes, the ability to ask questions of people in power, especially when it makes everybody feel awkward. You always look for the *elephant in the room* and address those issues. You need a level of detachment that allows you to continue your work. Like any job, you must learn to put the memories in a box and you do so perhaps by reading Harry Potter to your child at bedtime, going for a run, or cooking a family meal after work, no matter what kind of a day it has been.

Despite the coping strategies and attempts to switch off, there are people you meet for a short time that have a huge impact on your life, and your outlook. Their little faces, or their stories, will never leave you. Gillian Dempsey was one of those people.

When I met her in 2008, Gillian was a Third Class pupil in Scoil Mhichíl Naofa in Athy. Her teacher described her as 'sharing, caring and generous' and 'the bravest person I've ever known'.

The ten-year-old's classmates adored Gillian and wrote twenty-eight wonderful letters about her remarkable bravery. They prayed for her to get better, as she missed a lot of school suffering from lung and digestive problems, and early Cystic Fibrosis liver disease. She was constantly cared for by her parents, Elaine and Joe, and her siblings, Lauren and

Aaron. There was a warmth in Gillian's home that I will never forget. Years later, through my role as a presenter on local radio KCLR, I once again came across Gillian's older sister, Lauren Dempsey. Lauren also has Cystic Fibrosis but, thankfully, it is a milder form than her sister's.

Many of you may remember seeing Lauren as she stole our hearts when she went on her first ever date, but did it on national television. As a twenty-year-old media student Lauren went on *First Dates Ireland* and had us all on the edge of our seats as she confessed she had never been on a date before. She highlighted Cystic Fibrosis and tenderly remembered her sister on the programme.

Lauren was an amazing sister to Gillian, and you can tell that her little sister's short life has shaped the kind of person she has become today. During an interview with KCLR Live in April 2022, we connected Lauren with the 'wish granter' who helped her and Gillian's dreams come true many years back.

It was so clear that Make-A-Wish Ireland's ability to transform the sisters into princesses for the day was one of Lauren's stand-out memories with her sister. Lauren explained how those memories are so special now that Gillian is no longer here. She also fondly recalled how a 'big limousine' came to their house to collect them. They were dressed to the nines in their princess gowns that had arrived the week previously. The sisters, and their mum, Elaine, were whisked to Peter Mark in Dublin to get their hair done, and a trip to Debenham's ensued, where they were treated to a personal stylist to bring them shopping. Gillian was eight-years-old, Lauren was almost ten and those memories will stay with her forever. 'We were sent down to the GPO where there was a big horse and carriage waiting to bring us to afternoon tea,' she recalled.

The wish granter was Ailbhe Goff, and Lauren was surprised when we brought the two of them together for a radio interview to mark the thirtieth anniversary of Make-A-Wish Ireland. Local radio is such an emotive and powerful medium – I hadn't even realised our Make-A-Wish spokesperson was Gillian and Lauren's wish granter until it emerged during our live conversation. Lauren was also surprised to hear from Ailbhe, but it made the experience all the more special.

Gillian's life and premature death also had a profound effect on Ailbhe who admitted she kept an eye on Lauren on social media and kept in touch with her family as it was her 'first ever wish to grant'.

Even after she died, little Gillian's work to inspire and inform others with Cystic Fibrosis continued. Two years after she passed, Lauren and Aaron, became Ireland's youngest publishers by launching their late sister's book. Gillian wrote a story when she was just eight-years-old called 'Frogs of a Different Nature'. She wanted to explain to other children what they will experience with Cystic Fibrosis, and to reassure them not to be scared when they cough up 'frogs in their lungs'. The nurses had told Gillian when she was in hospital that they were only 'frogs of a different nature', and coughing helped to clear the lungs.

Even though her life was too short, brave Gillian Dempsey, the girl with the sixty-five roses is a little lady I will never forget.

DOWNHILL TO CHINA

Jack Gower

My story starts eighteen months before the 2022 Winter Olympics in Beijing. There was no national team programme for me to join that year and my partnership with other national teams had evaporated as Covid continued to make headlines around the world. Throughout the whole summer I had been working incredibly hard, and the time had finally come where I needed to head out to the mountains in order to commence my training on skis. The drive out to the mountains would take fourteen hours, and would be followed promptly by early mornings on the hill and tough workouts in the gym.

I was very nervous about the journey that lay ahead of me and conveyed this to my father. Fortunately, I managed to convince him to help with the drive, and then fly back home a few days later, on the premise that it would be a great chance to have some father and son bonding time. My father duly agreed, and with his three pairs of boxers and a couple of T-shirts we headed out to Switzerland.

Although the trip started by driving through the scenic Alps, it did not end that way! By the first day I had convinced Dad to help me for a short training block; this included waking up with me a four o'clock in the morning, heading up the hill and, after returning from training, preparing eight pairs of skis for the following days. At the end of the camp it became clear to me that I would not be able to complete my season without the ongoing help of my dad, who dutifully agreed to help with my endeavour.

We travelled the whole of Europe, taking part in the biggest ski races in the world. Together we took on, and competed with, teams with up to 30 members of staff helping their athletes. At first the whole mission of winning races was daunting for both of us, but in time we started to appreciate the incredible journey we were sharing together; laughing a lot and having a great time, all whilst competing in the World Cup.

The highlight of the trip came when we raced in Kitzbuhel, the most dangerous ski race in the world. Dad even got the opportunity to ski down the track (slowly). At the start we were both terrified, but we managed to survive the experience, which is one we now both hold dearly.

What started as a season where I was going to be by myself for the entire year, ended up being a season I got to spend with my dad. Everything about that year was difficult, but with the support I had from a small number of individuals it will be the season I will always remember. The next year I managed to partner up with a large national team and was proud to be chosen to represent my country in the Alpine Combined event – downhill and slalom – at the Beijing Olympics. I went on to claim the best result an Irish skier has achieved in Olympic history.

It's always important to be thankful for what, and who, you have; dark days shape you but looking back, they may not be so dark after all.

BEN, THE SHEEPDOG

Lt General Seán Clancy

Michael had been looking out over the high cliffs for nearly two hours now and could still just about see his new young sheepdog, Ben, about twenty metres below, stuck on a very narrow ledge and unable to move up or down. On the positive side, Michael thought, at least Ben hadn't moved an inch since he got stuck. It was as if this young and very excitable sheepdog had suddenly got a little sense. Just coming into view were Michael's friends on the Arun-class Lifeboat from Ballyglass. This was one of the bigger lifeboats on the West Coast and was going to stand-by in the water about 100 metres below Ben to support the rescue operation. Michael himself had been a volunteer on the lifeboat for many years, but this was a very unusual mission which he now had his friends involved in.

Michael lived on his farm in North Mayo and loved nothing more than to wander the fields with his trusted and obedient older sheepdog, Sam. Michael and Sam had been friends for nearly ten years and recently the time had come for Michael to start thinking about training a young dog in order to allow Sam take things a little easier and retire. Ben had joined them as a beautiful black and white collie pup only a couple of weeks earlier. Michael knew that the best way for Ben to learn the ropes was from Sam and for several weeks now the two of them had been hanging out together close to Michael's farmyard. Today was the first time Michael had decided that Ben was ready to gather the sheep near the cliffs.

Ben got off to a great start, watching how Michael and Sam worked together. Sam turned and twisted the sheep under Michael's whistle commands perfectly. After what seemed like forever, Ben was bursting with enthusiasm and when he noticed a few sheep who strayed away just at the edge of the cliffs he wanted to show Michael and Sam that he could do this himself and took off after the few strays. Ignoring Michael's whistles and Sam's barks, Ben bolted off frantically trying to show off his new skills. However, these sheep were old and crafty and seeing this new young pup running all over the place, they decided to take the pup for a tour of the cliffs to a point where Ben ended up twenty metres down the cliff edge, on a small ledge, from where he was unable to move up or down.

Michael was initially very cross but having seen many dangerous situations from his experience with the lifeboat, he knew straight away that this was not going to be an easy situation to resolve. Certainly, it was too risky to climb down to get Ben as the edge was very slippery and worn away by the sheep, not to mention the very heavy rain over the last few evenings. Michael was now the person who needed help and someone to rescue his new pup. First, he called out his pals in the Mayo Mountain Rescue who arrived at the cliff top shortly after the lifeboat was in position. The spot above where Ben had found himself was already very dangerous and was made even more so when combined with the very soft and difficult ground. As a result, everyone decided that it was not safe to proceed, putting people in danger and risking their lives to try and recover Ben. It was now looking very bad for Ben and for his owner Michael.

However, Michael had one last card up his sleeve and he called his friends in the helicopter Search and Rescue base in Finner Camp, County Donegal, who he knew were on their way to Blacksod Bay for a training exercise later that afternoon. The crew of the helicopter and the RNLI lifeboat had often trained together, so they knew each other well. It is important to train and practice together so that when an emergency arises everyone is prepared and ready to respond. Mind you, they never imagined they'd be working together to rescue a dog called Ben from a cliff!

When the helicopter arrived they initially hovered very high over the cliff where the helicopter crew could see Ben, who was scared and upset. So, after chatting with the Mountain Rescue team and Michael, they decided to winch their crewman, Lenny, onto the top of the cliff and walk him slowly down the cliff while still attached to the extended winch, which meant no weight on the cliff top, and no risk of falling rocks.

How Ben would react was the big unknown, and the big danger. If he got upset, excited or frightened by the helicopter he could easily fall. It took the crewman about ten minutes to walk very slowly down the cliff, stopping every so often to settle Ben. As Lenny approached Ben from the side he could see the dog was getting excited and when they were about a metre apart, Ben got so excited he leapt out to Lenny who managed to grab him by the neck and wrap his spare arm around him. Quickly the helicopter lifted them both back up to the top of the cliff and over the fields to safety.

As Ben reached the ground close to where everyone involved in the rescue was waiting, he leapt from Lenny's hands and ran around and around the field non-stop for what seemed like a lifetime while the lifeboat crews, the Mountain Rescue team, Michael and Sam looked on in amusement. Michael didn't bring Ben back to the upper fields near the cliffs again for a long time, but eventually Ben got sense, learned his skills and became a wonderful sheepdog, which finally allowed Sam to take it easy and retire.

Rescue crews are called upon to help people every day. Sometimes they even get called upon to very unusual situations but when it's for friends, it's great to get a positive result. Everyone involved in getting Ben to safety that day were so thrilled that it all ended so well. I know this because I was there as part of the helicopter crew.

EVERYTHING IS ALRIGHT TONIGHT

Anna Classon

All was well with the world as I turned in on the night of the 28 April 2010. I had recently undergone surgery and was pleased that my recovery was going well. As a Donegal woman I'm always more at home in the county of the Gaels, but on that particular night I was staying in Dublin with my in-laws and their support in my recovery was very much appreciated. I was happy, I was comfortable, and I was content; what could go wrong?

As a mother of four sons and the wife of a fisherman, there is always drama in my life. Our home, more often than not, resembles an airport departure gate; lots of leavings and arrivals and all the emotion that brings. I wouldn't have it any other way.

On that night, Ross, my husband, was somewhere off the north-west coast of Scotland and had earlier checked in to let me know he was fine, and the crab fishing was going well. I knew geographically where all my boys were and I had developed a habit of going to bed and, right before I laid my head down, saying to myself, 'Well, everything is alright tonight, Anna'. This mantra meant that there were no boys on the loose. In short, no rows or dramas on the horizon, and that suited me very well.

I work in the charity sector. Many people don't realise that the RNLI (Royal National Lifeboat Institution) is a charity, but it is, and I am so proud of the people whom I support through my role. They are life-savers and they are special. There is always a life to be saved, people on the water needing help, day and night. Perspective is something I am grateful for, and working with the lifeboat crews, I have it in spades. I have lost colleagues and friends from the fishing industry to the sea, so the magnitude of the work of the men and women in the RNLI is not lost on me.

At the time I was working as Fundraising and Communications Manager for Ireland. It's an interesting and a privileged position to be in, as you see things from the other side of a lifeboat callout. And let me tell you what I've learned – there is always hope in desperate situations, both from the families waiting quayside for any news, and from the rescuers who are out searching. There is always a belief that loved ones will come home safe, until time and the search tells you that the news is not good. It's then I see the rescuers assume new roles, as comforters and counsellors. They don't forget the ones who don't come home.

I was awoken at 6:00 a.m. on 29 April with a phone call from the Coastguard in Scotland. I'll never forget the words; 'There has been an incident with the MFV "Ainmire", no further information available at this time.' The MFV *Ainmire* was Ross's boat. I sat down in shock. What had happened? Where was Ross, my eldest son? Where was Christopher, my second son, who was also on the boat? Where was the crew? What was happening?

I worked for the RNLI, surely this was not happening to me? Silence and more silence. I was thinking, 'Who will I call?' I tried the boat's number but there was no reply. I tried the satellite phone and again there was no reply. I tried all the mobiles I could think of: nothing.

I turned on the radio. From past experience, the news sometimes carried information on searches for missing fishing crews. That morning was also the one where the death of Gerry Ryan, the much-loved broad-caster, was announced. It felt like a bad omen. A family somewhere was grieving. I sat like a zombie wondering what I was going to do. There was still no information from the Scottish Coastguard.

Finally, I phoned my sister Fiona. She lived in Drumcondra and came straight over to wait with me. I didn't fully realise it at the time, but this was exactly like all those times I had waited for news with other families. It was my turn and all my experience in this area counted for nothing. This one was personal, and it rendered me useless.

I now know that in the Operations Room of the RNLI, which is based in Poole, a discussion was taking place. They were aware of the situation. This was one of their own, they knew me, they knew the boat was my husband's, and they knew the crew were in trouble. They must have battled their own emotions but there was protocol that had to be followed and alerting me was not their role. They were aware that Stornoway Lifeboat had been launched, and that there were other boats in the area searching, but at the time I knew none of this.

The minutes waiting for the next phone call felt like hours. Then at last, the phone call came. All were saved, the boat was under tow, but she was sinking. We lost the boat that day but not the crew and not my family. They came home. It took a day or two, but home they came.

I think of that time so often; far more than I care to admit. That day was the day that I learned first-hand what it felt like to be the bystander in my own search and rescue drama, and I will never take the outcome for granted.

This is what we do, this is what the lifeboat crews do. These things doesn't just happen to other people, they happen to our people. I experienced so many emotions that day and I'm grateful for them all. Now, when I wait with a family or talk to the lifeboat crews who are out searching, I can honestly say, 'I know what you are feeling, and please don't give up'. Always hold on to hope and when it feels like hope is fading, as sometimes it will, let them take the strain, they know how to do it.

I will be forever grateful to the RNLI, an organisation I now head up in Ireland, to the UK Coastguard, and to the MFV *Our Hazel* for all they did that day to secure that outcome for me. They have given me the great gift to be able to say this evening as I turn into my bed, 'Well, everything is alright tonight, Anna'.

FOOD

JP McMahon

I have never told this story to anyone.

When I was younger, in my teenage years, I developed a difficult relationship with food. This was before I became a chef, or rather before I started cooking professionally. It's hard to imagine that someone who cooks their whole life might ever have had a difficult relationship with food, but it's true. This is because often the things that are right in front of us are the things that we cannot see.

I don't recall the specific time and place.

It just gradually developed.

I was always a little chubby as a child as this led to insults at home and in the school yard.

Fat was something that I did not want to be.

It was an insult, a horrible word.

But by the time I got to my teenage years, I really believed I was fat and grossly overweight.

To add insult to injury, I was also unfit.

Or at least not a fit as the rest of the boys in my school.

I remember sometime around the age of fourteen coming second last in a one-mile race at school.

The trauma was awful.

The stigma.

I resolved to change things and began training myself to run.

First a mile, and then two.

Then it was three and then four.

By the time I got to Fifth Year at school, I was running six to eight miles every morning before school.

I ran 10 km in 36 minutes.

I had achieved what I set out to do.

But the difficulty with food never went away.

I would count calories obsessively, jotting them down in a little notebook, making sure I didn't eat too much; though always allowing for the fact that on the days I ran I could eat more.

Huge bowls of pasta.

Lots and lots of yoghurts.

Peanut butter toasted sandwiches.

Lots and lots of food.

However, in spite of how much I ran, the feeling of fatness never went away. I always seem to remain the same shape.

Running more and more and feeling the same.

Fat and inadequate.

So, I decided to start cutting back on food.

I tried to eat less and less each day.

It got to the point where I didn't have enough energy to run because I wasn't eating enough.

My weight had dropped to eight stone twelve pounds.

I was around eighteen.

I thought I would be happy, but I wasn't.

I wanted to run and I wanted food.

So, I started to eat a lot and then make myself sick.

Loads of ice-creams.

Loads of chocolate bars.

Then I would make myself sick.

My throat hurt.

But I couldn't tell anyone.

I was ashamed and I couldn't speak.

Ashamed into silence.

I just kept it to myself and went about my day, counting calories, starving myself, feeding myself, making myself sick.

I don't know how long this went on for.

Probably from the age of fourteen to twenty.

I honestly cannot remember.

I suppose one day the urge just went away.

I stopped making myself sick.

It didn't mean that I stopped bingeing. Eating lots and then starving myself again. Or it didn't mean that the shame, the depression, or the anxiety dissipated.

It was all still there.

I drank to suppress my panic.

But when I started cooking professionally, my relationship with food changed somewhat.

I regulated myself better.

It doesn't mean that over 25 years later, I still don't think about these things.

I do.

And I often stand in front of the mirror and wonder why I am so fat. I often eat too much. I often eat too little.

But the relationship I have with food now is a more holistic one.

I'm a chef.

I educate people about food, about how to cook good food, especially children. I run three restaurants and a cookery school. From the outside, it seems as if my life is perfect, even though it often isn't.

People say to me that I've made it; that my life is sorted.

Life is never sorted.

It is an ongoing, open process that never stops.

I don't know why I told you this story.

Perhaps it was to free myself from some of my demons.

Or maybe it was to make you, the reader, realise that the old adage, 'Never judge a book by its cover', rings true.

Many feel my life is some golden beacon.

I am a famous chef.

And of course, I shine the light that I have created on as many people as possible.

But that doesn't mean that I don't live exactly like everyone else.

Day to day.

Often struggling, often overcoming.

When you meet someone for the first time, be kind.

As you never know what trouble bubbles inside them.

We are all an assemblage of contradictions, sometimes both happy and sad simultaneously.

It's okay not to know, not to know what to do, not to know what you want, and not to be able to stop.

Because there are people around you that you can reach out to talk to when you need to.

My ten-year-old daughter often asks my what you can do for free.

And I answer: 'You can smile and talk to someone.'

My Summer County Complex

Joe Duffy

Mother would never let Summer County cross the door, let alone grace our kitchen table.

After all, it was *margarine*.

So, of a Thursday when money was running low, very low, and it still being a day – and a night – away from my father's weekly wage packet, we would be despatched to Ruane's shop for a quarter pound of butter. Not the much cheaper, half pound of Summer County. Never. Ever.

To be seen with margarine would be mortification. An indication of inability to cope, like waving a white flag to the poverty that was constantly knocking at the hall door.

As if I would draw attention to myself running the short distance from our house on one side of Claddagh Green to the shop on the other, doing a three-hand reel with the dreaded gold-foil-wrapped, exotically-titled margarine; at least the quarter of butter was wrapped discreetly in greaseproof paper, and hidden.

Bizarrely, Mother seemed to lose her fear of social embarrassment when it came to the dreaded trips to the turf depot. A trip that involved a three-mile trek through the centre of Ballyfermot with my little brother Aidan's pram, laden with teetering sacks of wet turf. A marching band in full flight would attract less attention than me and my younger brother Peter trying to manhandle Aidan's pram up Ballyfermot Road – which in truth is a long, punishing, steep hill rather than an innocuous road.

Not only did she drop all social pretence when it came to the quest for turf, she seemed to forget other basic principles of family life which I firmly held to, such as the eldest should be called on first for the heavy jobs.

It was probably because James, our eldest, was already working with my father in Glen Abbey Hosiery and handing up his unopened brown wage packet every Friday, and so was granted an amnesty from this backbreaking, public toil.

And of course, everyone knew that to go to the turf depot was a sign that times were tough in your house – after all, only poor old age pensioners were given the 'turf dockets'. Which is where we got ours, our Nana Murphy being the entitled bearer of the hand-written yellow scraps of paper, grandly titled 'Fuel Vouchers', granting the bearer 'one hundredweight of turf', which gave our family heat and life, but instilled nothing but dread into my heart.

Because I knew, once the docket was safely placed in mother's purse it would not be long before she would noisily drag Aidan's pram from its parking spot under the stairs, throw the two empty coal sacks in, and call myself and Peter to order, before nonchalantly directing us to the turf depot, with a rider that not a single sod was to be lost by theft or negligence on the way back.

I refuse to believe that the same woman who saw nothing but embarrassment in being seen with a half-pound of foil-wrapped margarine was immune to the stigma of her two young sons wrestling with two four-stone, carbuncled, dirty sacks of turf stacked high on their baby brother's pram, pushing and willing it three miles up Ballyfermot's main road.

The Saint Patrick's Day parade going up O'Connell Street would crane fewer necks and turn fewer heads.

The run to the turf depot on Lally Road was long, but it was downhill after all – and the pram was empty, but still our hearts filled with fear once we turned right on to O'Hogan Road because it was then we would see the length of the queue. Hundreds of other – bigger – kids, standing there with every class of vehicle from boxcar to bicycle, all queueing for the turf. Not only was it the fear of being beaten up by these kids, who might discover that we were from the *top end* of the scheme, that sent our hearts racing, it was the prospect of a wasted journey if the turf ran out before we got to the top of the queue.

And so we stood, silently, fuming, fearful, as the queue of wheeled contraptions snaked its way up Lally Road to the turf depot. The depot, by the way, was no more than a yard with an antiquated weighing scales on a wooden frame at its centre. When we got to the top of the queue we would hand over our golden docket to the shovel-man, who would heave the appropriate cast iron metal weight onto the scales. Shovelling turf in the open-mouthed metal scoop, you were instructed to hold your coal sack as the gangly, unruly sods flew in every direction – except into your sack.

It was like trying to wrestle an octopus into a net bag.

We would be laughed at, sneered at, and jeered at, as Peter and myself – amateurs – scrambled to fill the sacks and manhandle them onto the pram. We scurried off as quickly as possible, shaking off any potential cowboys from the lower end of the scheme who might attempt to rustle our precious pile.

The most difficult part of the climb was the beginning. It was not just the steep hill that challenged us, we would be humiliated if by chance any of our teachers were leaving our school as we skulked past, for surely they would spot us trying to roll our boulder, like Sisyphus, up the unending Ballyfermot Hill.

Peter and I would take turns gripping and pushing the white rubber clad handle of the pram – the effort rendering us almost horizontal

– while the other would push from the side and stop it from rolling back down the hill. But neither of us could let up, or let go.

We beat a steady path, shifting from the shadows only once when *go-be-the-wall*, the local walking book reader, headed straight in our direction and refused to deviate – as always.

And we dared not give up. We always did what Mother told us, since the time she caught myself and Peter mitching from school. Well, actually we gave ourselves up after two hours of boredom, our stuttering excuse that the school was closed expiring within seconds as Mother's instinct reduced us to a pair of blubbering truth-tellers. Propelling us up the stairs to our bedrooms by the robust application of a wooden spoon to the back of our legs as an effective, and memorable, sanction.

And so, we could not even contemplate surrender. We did our best. Gathering extra wind as we got to the main row of shops, not because of a nasty incline, but because it was where the Duffy brothers were most likely to be spotted by passing neighbours on the top deck of the 78-bus home.

Neither was our arrival home worthy of a remark by either our mother or siblings. For Peter and myself we had just completed a feat comparable only to Edmund Hillary and Tenzing Norgay ascending Mount Everest thirteen years previously, except they had more oxygen.

After emptying the sacks of turf into the coal shed, the two of us would clean out Aidan's pram and, as sure as anything, Mother would remind us that we were not to go out to play without the pram and its rightful occupant, baby Aidan, in his command and control position, in the middle of the pram.

This lack of gratitude baffled us no end.

Mother – who died in her ninety-third year, in 2022 – still remembered and abided by the Summer County fatwa, but had no recollection of our epic turf expeditions.

Unremarked upon then, and now. A life lesson.

You see, Mother believed the greater gift of humility and the lesson that *life can be hard but bearable* comes from overcoming the bigger challenge.

Sure, who would notice a young fella carrying a half pound of Summer County margarine anyway?

In memory of Mabel Duffy 1929–2022

HOPE AND INSPIRATION

Cathy Kelly

The plane was full and I, in a window seat near the back, had the row to myself. I'm a neat traveller and had settled myself in with my bag stowed carefully and a book on my lap.

We hadn't long to go before the flight from the UK to Dublin was due to take off, so I looked at the cover of my book blankly.

I began pondering how precisely my row was empty when the rest of the plane was jammed and at that moment, an elderly gentleman handed an elderly lady in a bright pink cardigan into the seat beside me.

She was pretty, with large eyes, probably in her late seventies, with curled grey hair and the sort of face that spoke of much smiling in life.

She smiled at me now and began looking for her seatbelt.

'I can't find it!' she said, with sudden and clearly mounting anxiety and as she leaned forward, searching, her husband, a man with kind eyes, looked at me from his seat on the outside of our row and mouthed the word 'dementia.'

I understood instantly.

My father, over twenty-three years dead now, had early-onset dementia.

I was all too familiar with the dance of the carer when they bring their beloved somewhere, a dance where the carer plucks spoons and other things from the person's pockets because those with dementia often inadvertently take on the role of a pickpocket as if they were at home. There's no badness in this.

Simply, they become fascinated with things, have an urgent need to take an item and put it safely away, because their brain is telling them this is the right thing to do.

Their poor brain, awareness sometimes there and sometimes not, is being cruelly eroded and slowly losing the ability to exist in the world.

In that moment, with the lady in pink beside me, I was brought back to my mother and I taking my father places.

As is the case with some neurological diseases, he looked perfectly fine but he wasn't.

To preserve his dignity, one of us would link his arm and the other would run ahead or stay behind to explain.

At the voting centre, I ran ahead to explain that my mother would have to stand in the little ballot box with him, even though it wasn't allowed. My father always voted. He knew there was an election and it was vitally important to him to vote.

I don't think he knew who was in the election. But vote he would and we were there to help him.

Bouncing back into the present, I turned to the lady in pink who was worrying about her seat belt.

'Let me help you', I said.

I found her seatbelt and engaged in a long chat about how seatbelts were tricky things and hid themselves.

'Yes,' she said, delightedly.

Her husband mouthed 'thank you'.

Airports are trying and it's always a long way to walk, we agreed.

But there would be tea soon.

Her bracelets were pretty, I said, and she told me about them.

CATHY KELLY

It is strange the things that remain clear as a bell in the mind.

Her husband, whom I shall call Jim, cast me a happy look. I understood. He could relax.

His wife, Jill, was happy because we were safe in our seats, her beloved husband beside her and this strange woman was chatty and kind.

How important it is to be kind.

And we began to talk, the three of us, in one of those conversations you can have with a person with dementia when two of you know what to do and want to take care of this beautiful soul.

Jill was such a darling person. Four children, all grown up and one living in Ireland, which was where they were going. Grandchildren too.

Jill and Jim lived in the UK and their accents made me think they were from up the northernmost reaches in Scotland.

But they weren't.

Jim, who spoke with the same accent as his wife, was Irish.

He'd left Ireland when he was eighteen.

Only a few pennies in his pocket but he needed to leave. And in the UK, he found his beloved wife. They were married, I think, 60 years.

At this, he patted her hand with love.

'*Never a cross word,*' he said.

Four sons, Jill said again, beaming. The son in Ireland was the only one with Irish hair, she said, like his father.

I love hearing people's stories but I wasn't going to ask why he'd left. To work, like so many Irish people over the years, I assumed.

Yes and no.

Jim began to talk about what had sent him away.

At the age of seven, he'd been put in an industrial school.

I knew the name and I shivered. I have driven past what there is of the industrial school in Letterfrack and it makes me shiver with the pain that emerges from it, like a miasma of suffering that defies time.

Without getting angry or bitter, this gentle grandfather talked about physical abuse and punishments, about the fear, about how some children – not him, but many of the boys he knew – were abused in a way he wouldn't even speak about.

When he was sixteen, he was told to leave and sent, without any money, to a family business to work as what sounded like an indentured servant.

After two years, he left with almost no money and the clothes he stood up in.

He left Ireland and had the wonderful fortune to meet Jill, to start a new life with this warm woman and to have a family he adored.

The industrial school was there in his head, he said. But he had so much. Family. Grandchildren. His beloved Jill.

He – and some old friends – had been to the Residential Institutions Redress Board in the earliest days of its existence and had felt hurt, humiliated, misunderstood.

Some of the boys he knew, now men, would never recover from it all.

But he – and he held onto Jill's hand, the hand that was soft from his rubbing hand cream into it – was lucky.

If everyone has a book in them, then Jim has many. But he has something far greater: love, hope, joy, and must be an inspiration to all who meet him. He and Jill were travelling to the country he should loathe but he was smiling, carefully caring for his wife, his innate goodness and determination to find joy spreading out of him like rays of the sun.

I've changed their names so their story is private, but I think of them a lot.

How life can deal a person one hand of cards and how they can play that hand in a way that most of us can barely imagine. He was inspirational.

A Remarkable Young Lady

Brendan Power

Christmas was exciting, as it always is when there are young children involved. For us it was our grandchildren, and we had the best time of our lives watching their faces as they opened their presents, leaving a trail of wrapping paper for us to collect. Playing with the new toys had to be interrupted at one point when Christmas dinner was served, but fortunately there were a few items that were small enough to bring to the table. Saint Stephen's day was crisp and cold, but it was dry, and taking their new bikes into the countryside was the order of the day.

We lived next door to my son and his family and were surprised, then shocked, later in the evening when our grandson came running in to tell us that his sister was having a fit. We ran back with him to find her semi-conscious in her dad's arms and totally unresponsive to anything we said, or did. An ambulance rushed her to hospital where, after various tests and scans, she was diagnosed with a brain tumour – astrocytoma – and our world would never be the same again. She was just seven years old.

Within 48 hours of the diagnosis, she underwent surgery to have the tumour removed, but it would be a further 24 hours before we were allowed to visit her; without doubt the longest 24 hours of my life. I didn't know quite what to expect when I walked in to the hospital ward, but the terrifying sight of stiches on her scalp, and the various pipes, monitors and cannulas attached to her, was neutralised somewhat by the huge smile on her face.

'Guess what Granddad? I've had an operation.' I tried hard to match her smile but, of course, nobody could do that; Niamh always had the biggest and brightest of smiles, bright enough to light up even the darkest days.

The surgeon pronounced the operation a success, but another week in hospital would still be necessary to aid her recovery and allow more tests to be carried out. Although confined to bed for most of the day, she spent much of her time offering encouragement to other children in the ward, seemingly oblivious to her own problems.

At home she was still weak and, disappointingly for her, unable to attend school where she had always enjoyed learning and discovering new things, and where, just a few weeks earlier, she had been elected by her peers to represent her year on the school council. A private tutor was made available for a few hours a week at the hospital, and whilst this provided a much needed, and welcome, break in her routine, it wasn't quite the same.

After a month or so she started radiotherapy sessions which further weakened her, but eventually she was well enough to go back to school for a few half days each week. One evening she sent us a little note to say she was 'going to school for a full day tomorrow'. Of course, we went to see her straight away and I don't think I've ever seen anyone as excited about anything, and – if it was possible – I'm sure her wonderful smile was even bigger than usual.

For a while, even if it was just for one day, she could be the same as the other children, doing her schoolwork and playing with her friends, but it exerted a heavy toll on her and by the end of the day she was exhausted. That did nothing to lessen her excitement, however, or her smile and her enthusiasm, which gripped us all as she told us everything about her day, before eventually succumbing to her tiredness and falling asleep.

Her parents, Simon and Marie, made the decision to give up work in order to take care of her, and did everything they could to make her life as normal as possible, and to help her through her ordeal. A short break on the Yorkshire coast was followed by a couple of weeks in our house on the Hook Peninsula, and shortly after her eighth birthday she took her First Communion.

Perhaps I was in denial, but to me Niamh appeared to be improving so it came as a huge blow when we heard the cancer had returned and a second operation would be necessary. Chemotherapy was needed after that, leaving her constantly tired and weak, so school was off the agenda again and now the private tutor visited her at home. The thing she loved most, and looked forward to, during this time, was when her school friends, twins Isabelle (Issy) and Amelia, came to visit. For a while she could forget everything else and just be a normal little girl again, laughing and joking and sharing secrets. Issy was her best friend, perhaps the best friend anybody could ever have, and when they were together nothing else seemed to matter.

Seb, her big brother, just two years older but mature beyond his years, found his own life on pause during her illness. They had always been very close and loved each other's company, and her smile seemed to get even bigger when he was around. Simon and Marie worked hard – as did we – to keep things on an even keel for him but, despite our best efforts, it was inevitable that he would often have to take second place as everybody's energy was directed towards aiding Niamh's recovery. It was the number one priority for all of us and throughout her illness he never once complained, seeming to take it in his stride, bearing everything with incredible fortitude and showing a strength of character that would put many of his elders to shame. I could not have been more proud of him.

To say we were devastated would be the understatement of the century, when a scan showed the tumour had returned and a third operation would be necessary. Nobody ever said life was fair, but this was way beyond that. This time the operation did not go as well as the previous two, with Niamh suffering a stroke during the procedure. Her left arm was virtually unusable and she needed leg braces to help her learn to walk again but, although the muscles in her face were affected, her smile was still there and for me it was brighter than ever. I was learning a lot about courage from this little girl as she faced her challenges with a level of stoicism and determination I could only aspire to. There would be no more school for some time now but she still had the services of a tutor.

Every night I had the joy of reading a story to her, with Seb joining us to listen in. When we'd finished, we would pick a story for the following night and, just from the title, we each had to hazard a guess as to what it was about. It was clear that Niamh's imagination was still as vivid as ever and her forecasts were invariably better than ours, and very often better than the story itself.

Her recovery was progressing well, her walking was improving and she had adapted to cope with the difficulties that had been inflicted on her when a routine scan showed the tumour was back, and, even worse, it was terminal.

The consultant said he could, and would, perform another operation, but the decision had to be made by her parents. If the operation went ahead, he explained, it would extend her life (for exactly how long, he couldn't say) but at a very high cost. There would be no improvement in her quality of life, it would involve further trauma, and we would be doing it for us rather than for her.

Simon and Marie were in an impossible situation; not one that any parent should have to face, and one that required considerable thought. Having spoken to Niamh, who was adamant she did not want another operation, they showed unbelievable courage and incredible love when they made the completely selfless decision not to put her through any further stress. I am forever grateful that I did not have to make such a decision; I don't know if I would have been brave enough, or if I would have been too selfish, to do the right thing.

Knowing she would only be with them for another six months or so, they were determined to use every minute of that time to keep searching for a cure, to make her life as enjoyable as possible, and to create memories that would never fade.

The first of those memories came a few weeks before Christmas when Make-A-Wish flew her to Lapland, with her mother, where she had a magical time and got to meet Father Christmas – 'the real one, granddad', she told me when she returned home. She must have been right, because on Christmas morning all the presents she'd asked him for were there waiting for her under the tree.

A Harley Street specialist recommended her for clinical trials of a new drug, which saw her spend a week in hospital, sadly without success. When she came out she brought with her a beautiful picture she had made for me as a St Patrick's day gift; not surprisingly it now adorns the wall of my study.

A very good friend arranged a special treat for her in London, where she met the members of One Direction, her favourite group. When they walked into the room her eyes lit up, and then she broke down in tears. They must have been tears of joy because she later told us that it was 'the best day of my life'.

Easter on the Hook Peninsula saw her hunting for Easter eggs, building sandcastles and enjoying art lessons with Rose at the lighthouse. A couple of nights before the end of the holiday, after reading her a story, I asked her if she wanted to say a prayer, and suggested she use her own words. 'Dear God, please make by arm work properly, like the other one, and please don't let me have any more operations. Amen.' If my heart wasn't broken before, it certainly was then. It was the first, and only, time I had ever heard her express any form of self-pity.

A few weeks later we celebrated her ninth birthday in the company of her friends and family by spending a few days in Center Parcs. She had a wonderful time, insisting on getting involved in all the activities, but it was very tiring for her and when she started to feel unwell, her parents took her home, and then on to Bluebell Wood Children's Hospice, where she would spend the next six weeks. It was a marvellous facility where she had spent some time before, and where the wonderful, caring, staff always went above and beyond.

On Friday, 6 July I had an early morning meeting in the office, during which my phone rang. It was Simon, calling to tell me that at one minute past seven, Niamh had passed away. She had died peacefully snuggled in the arms and loving embrace of her mummy and daddy.

In the church, just a few hundred yards from her school, there were so many people at her funeral that it was standing room only. TV, radio and press reporters, who had all followed her story over the past twelve months, were there for the final chapter, and police were needed to control the traffic.

The emptiness I felt then is still with me today and although she is no longer with us in person, she lives on forever in my thoughts and in my heart, and there is not a single day when my memories of her don't bring a tear to my eye, or a smile to my lips. I have now come to understand the adage that says: *grief is the price we pay for love.*

I often wonder what Niamh would have been like as a teenager and how she would have progressed in life, but, sadly, that is something none of us will never know. What I do know is that for the nine short years she was here she made a difference, she had a positive influence on many of those around her, and she taught us all what courage really is.

Truly, a remarkable young lady.

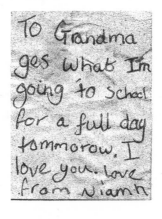

Love and Courage

Des Kenny

During the early 1980s, as a member of the Galway Lions Club, I was asked by its president, who happened to be my brother Tom, to take over a new project, which was to send a monthly cassette to the visually impaired people of Galway.

The idea was first mooted by the language laboratories of Galway University (NUIG) whose director, Seán MacIomhar, would record the cassette and arrange its distribution. The Lions Club was to organise its content, and because it was for the blind and visually impaired, postage was free.

My daunting job was to organise the content. After a number of meetings with Seán MacIomhar, we decided to base this on the relatively new, free Galway newspaper, the *Galway Advertiser*. It was to have local news, sports, music and features, and our aim was to have at least twelve different voices on every issue. We called it the *Galway Echo* and it lasted more than twenty years.

Compiled by BRENDAN POWER

The first issues were tentative, to say the least, but gradually, thanks to the expertise, patience and knowledge of Seán MacIomhar, it did take shape, and became an important part of my life. From the very beginning, I learnt a great deal about what it meant to be blind, and what the *Galway Echo* should be.

Sometime during the first year of the *Echo* (as we came to call it), the door of the bookshop opened and Peter O'Toole, the actor, walked in. Born in Connemara, he had often been in the shop and Mother welcomed him warmly. As he was wandering through the bookshop and art gallery, I began to wonder if he would come on the *Echo*. After agonising over this for a good five or ten minutes, I rang Seán Mac-Iomhar to see if he was available. He was and so I approached this icon of the stage and screen, told him about the tape and nervously asked him for an interview. His answer took me by surprise, 'That will cost you'. I regained my composure and was about to launch into a spiel about this being a charitable organisation, when he continued, '… a cup of coffee', which, of course, was provided immediately.

Thus began what was to become a major feature of the *Echo*: the interview. Anybody and everybody who was somebody, and who visited the bookshop and art gallery, was approached. Very few, if any, refused. Christy Moore called anytime he was in town ('Are you still doing that gig?'), Siobháin McKenna, Seamus Heaney, John McGahern, Paddy Moloney of the Chieftains and Des O'Malley, just after he had inaugurated the Progressive Democrats. Commander Bill King, who was a much-decorated captain of a submarine during the Second World War, gave us a graphic description of life underwater in the Pacific and the North Atlantic, whilst a blind man described how his guide dog had guided him safely out of the Twin Towers when they were under attack during 9/11. There is, however, one interview that remains planted firmly in my memory, and stands head and shoulders above all the others in terms of love and courage.

It was with a German lady – whom we will call Renate – who had been a senior manager in a factory in East Germany, before the reunification of the country. Heinrich – another fictitious name – was a commercial traveller from the West who regularly visited Renate's factory on business. They got to know each other and over time they fell in love, but in the pervading culture of fear where everybody was watching everybody, their relationship was soon spotted and reported to the powers that be. Such liaisons, with people from the West, were forbidden by the communist authorities, and she was demoted to the factory floor.

Heinrich continued to visit the factory on business but was being watched carefully, which meant their clandestine affair became more and more difficult to pursue. Eventually a baby was born, making the constant separation even harder for them both. Each time they parted, they knew it could be for the last time as the authorities could ban Heinrich from the country at any time. They decided to make a break for the West; it would be dangerous but their love was so strong they believed it would see them through.

All of this was narrated to me in halting English, which added tension to the narrative.

On his next trip from West Germany, Heinrich sneaked Renate and the baby on to the back seat of the car and headed west before her absence was spotted, and reported to the dreaded Stasi (the state secret police). Traffic on the roads was very sparse, allowing them to pull off in an isolated spot before they got too close to the border. They were now about to enter the most dangerous part of their escapade as Renate got out of the car with the baby and climbed into the boot. As they continued on their journey the tension in the car was almost physical.

The ominous sight of the border crossing with its little collection of buildings hove into Heinrich's sight and, as he approached it, he was horrified to discover that the same border guard who had passed him through that morning was still on duty. Would he question him as to why he was returning so soon? Would he want to search the car? There was nothing he could do now but hope and pray.

Inside the boot, as Renate lay as still as possible, with her arm around the sleeping baby, she could hear snatches of a conversation. Then – she remembers as though it was yesterday – the sound of footsteps echoing on the cobbles as the guard started walking slowly towards the back of the car, step by step. She prepared herself for the worst, knowing that if he opened the boot it would be all over; she would never see her husband, or her child, again. She hardly dared to breathe as she clasped her baby to her breast, waiting for the shout that would signal her discovery, and then …

And then the footsteps stopped, for an eternal minute.

They started again …

But this time they were retreating, towards the front of the car.

In the driver's seat, Heinrich was doing his best to put on a show of indifference and could hardly believe his eyes when the guard waved him through the barriers.

To freedom.

The freedom we all take for granted.

Life Goes On

Nicola Tallant

I walked to the door of my artisan cottage in the heart of Dublin's Liberties. The knocking had been intense and had made me jump. I was expecting to find one of my neighbours brandishing a bottle of wine, or with a request for a visitor to park up outside my home.

We were an eclectic bunch of blow-ins that lived at Reginald Square just off Meath Street. I, for one, had paid far too much for the tiny house having hunted for months for a period property to do up before finally realising I couldn't afford one. The ever-increasing prices in the late 1990s meant that for a while I was the talk of the Liberties for what I'd paid for the cottage – until of course another one outpriced it.

For a twenty-something it was a cool little cottage, built in the late 1800s by the Dublin Artisans' Dwelling Company, founded by the great philanthropist Sir Edward Cecil Guinness. There was a mezzanine bedroom and a small backyard which I'd painted pink and decorated with lights and trinkets.

The houses all faced one another and my neighbours were a collection of young buyers like myself, divorcees and those who ran bespoke businesses in the city. One had a pen shop, another designed scarves and the legendary Irish musician Tony MacMahon had two of the cottages, which he had knocked together. His was the party house and he regularly called in at all hours, often getting me up out of bed, with the exciting news that the Dubliners were in his home and a session was starting. 'Bring what you have in the house,' he'd roar, meaning drink. The late Barney McKenna was the star and we'd all bundle in with wine and beer and whatever else we had in our cupboards and enjoy the magic until the sun rose.

Kathleen was the only local, an elderly woman who'd spent her life at home, foregoing marriage to mind her mother as she aged. Once a year she'd travel to Lourdes, but she loved a good session and a brandy. It was my job to escort her to and from Tony's, and she'd often get teary-eyed to the strains of 'On Raglan Road' or 'Down by the Sally Gardens'.

I pulled open the door but instead of a familiar face there was a gathering of children stood in formation with a dog-eared copybook and a pen. The oldest, who stood behind the smaller ones, explained that they were collecting money for a school fundraiser, that they'd be conducting a sponsored skiathlon and that the money was going to a good cause.

I went into the house and took twenty quid from my wallet. It was a lot but I'd no change and, after all, this was my neighbourhood now and I had to contribute to the community.

The same group called at Christmas, carol singing very badly in heavy Dublin accents and with their older sibling behind corralling them like goats.

By February they were collecting for a new wall at the school and in March they'd organised a whip-around for a school tour, to the zoo they said. When they knocked in April to announce a twenty-four-hour sponsored silence I knew there was something amiss. I handed over the money but watched them from the window as they made their way around the square.

Tony didn't answer. He was probably away on one of his tours. The man on the corner, who was a company director and drove a big Mercedes, handed them something and quickly closed the door. The scarf woman too paid up and they cleaned up from other neighbours too. The older one kept the money and urged them to stand to attention as they awaited the big wooden doors to swing open. As I watched a little one went to knock on Kathleen's door but was quickly swept away. And then they were off, out from the square and towards Meath Street, their pockets full, their faces set in mischievous grins.

Some years later in Albania, on the Kosovan border, I picked my way through ice-covered craggy hillsides where tens of thousands of refugees were making the crossing to escape war. A child holding the hand of a little one walked barefoot across the jagged rocks, her feet red and tinged blue. Us journalists had the best gear that money could buy and one reached down and removed the thermal socks from her feet to give to the child. She'd plenty more in her backpack, she said. The rest of us fumbled for money and whatever we had. Later in the week I saw her again, barefoot in the snow, and watched her gratefully thank a volunteer for the shoes and socks that had been specially sourced for her then scuttle off to add them to her pile. I often wondered where she is today, and how many pairs of Laboutins are in her wardrobe.

In the Philippines, on assignment in a red-light district where young girls cost sex tourists just ten dollars a night, a child selling flowers sat on a bar stool beside me to chat. 'What do you want to do when you grow up?' I asked. 'I want to be a doctor,' he said. Impressed, I found enough money to make his eyes bulge and told him to keep it all, to put it into his education fund. When three more of the flower sellers cited the same career dreams I knew that again I'd been had, but perhaps one made it.

Years after I'd moved out of Reginald Square and rented the house, I returned with a border collie called Jessica who was much more suited to the new house with a garden we'd lived in until the current renovations had started. The Liberties had changed, or maybe I had. There was something in the air, a menace, but my four-legged friend didn't notice.

She was a lesser spotted canine in the city centre and thus enjoyed a certain celebrity status. She liked to wander and let herself in to other people's houses. And I would regularly have to go out and look for her to bring her home. She was particularly fond of a Rastafarian man who spent his days smoking weed, listening to really cool music and generally enjoying life. I'd find them in an embrace on the floor of the living room and have to coax her out. Her other spot was in the local chipper, behind the counter, where customers would direct their orders at her. Nobody found it disgusting, despite the carpets of hair she seemed to shed on a daily basis. I was wrong about the place; the Liberties still had its charms. It was just irreverent and it loved a chancer, just like the kids who used to come to my door with their tall tales.

I saw the girl one day. The older one who ran the childish racket to fleece the blow-ins. No longer a kid but not yet an adult she was pushing a buggy, another baby in her belly, a cigarette in her hand. She looked haunted, wasted and all out of tricks. Children certainly have an incredible resilience for what the world throws at them and wherever they are they can hustle with the best. But at some point, for many, that stops being fun. And at some point they realise that the small windfalls simply aren't enough. Those who give the money, go away without ever asking who they are. They disappear into a crowd or out of a neighbourhood to never be seen again.

And life just goes on. And childhood ends.

REACH FOR THE STARS

Tommy Fleming

Each one of us has a story to tell. Each one of us has faced or, at some point in our life, will face a challenge of some description. For many, that challenge will seem daunting and hopeless and this is why I want to share my story and hope it gives courage to those who face adversity in their lives.

I firmly believe that we all hold within us the strength to deal with, and overcome, many difficult situations. I don't for one minute suggest that it is easy to do so, but believe me when I say that it is possible, and so very worthwhile to give it your best shot.

Let me take you back to the very early days of my career, which had finally started to take off after many years traipsing the long lonesome road of a wannabe singing star. I was a determined young fella – still am determined, just not quite so young. I kept knocking and knocking and knocking, and eventually the doors started to open.

My big break came when I was spotted performing with a quartet called *Jarog* at an open-air festival in Westport, Co Mayo in 1993. Within months, under the wing of the legendary Phil Coulter, I was touring America and Canada, walking out onto the great stages of the Boston Symphony and Carnegie Halls.

Before I knew it, I was touring worldwide with *Dé Danann* and it was 'game on' for Tommy Fleming. I was now playing with the big boys, and loving every minute of it. I was a grafter; I worked hard and was proud to release my first solo album, *Restless Spirit*, in 1996.

In the music business, when you release an album you take that album on tour, which can span twelve months or longer. At that time I had one goal in mind – a solo career, and I was totally focused on that. The album and tour did well and included a cover of a Clifford T Ward song, 'The Best Is Yet To Come', a personal favourite of mine to this day. Just keep that title in your mind for now while you join me on the next part of my story.

So, there I was – a young buck, the youngest of a family of six, from Aclare up beyond Lough Talt in Co Sligo – working my way up the steep ladder of the music industry, and doing pretty good for myself. The world was my oyster, and as far as I was concerned, I was unstoppable. I had plans, big plans, and even though I was in the middle of a busy promotional tour for my first album, ideas for my next album were whirling round in my never idle head as I drove home.

It was late enough. I was tired and hungry and anxious to get home and I decided to take a shortcut! A decision that resulted in a life changing major car accident.

Veering off the road I lost control of the steering and I collided with a tree, fair going for someone who fifteen minutes earlier had thought himself unstoppable. I lost consciousness for some time. I still have no idea for how long.

Although in severe pain having sustained serious injuries, when I came to my survival instincts kicked in. I hauled my bruised and battered body through a window literally at the very second the car burst into flames. I was absolutely petrified. It was late, dark, cold and very much off the beaten track. Somehow, I managed to stagger for about two miles before, thankfully, being picked up by a local couple who brought me home.

That's when the panic set in. The doctor was called, the ambulance arrived, the whole shebang. A swift examination at Castlebar General Hospital confirmed that my neck was broken and I was immediately transferred to the Mater Hospital in Dublin where they fitted me with a 'Jerome Halo' – a steel brace, fitted to your shoulders, encasing your head/neck and literally held in place with screws into either side of your forehead.

I spent many long dark days brooding in hospital fearing the answers to so many questions, mainly 'would I be paralysed?' Could this be the end of my career? Doctors were debating surgery – which could have damaged my vocal cords. I wondered which was worse, to not be able to walk or to not be able to sing, or even both. I was, quite honestly, in a heap.

Those first few days, while my condition was being assessed, every fear I ever had played a relentless tune on a permanent loop in my head. Those were dark days, days I will never ever forget. Those were days when I genuinely thought that Tommy Fleming would never again see, or be seen in, the spotlight.

There was lots of time to reflect during those early days in the spinal injury unit and I admit I wallowed in a haze of self-pity, something that was totally uncharacteristic of me. In retrospect I have accepted that it was all part of processing my situation. So, yes, I wallowed for a spell but that changed when I met a brave young man, also striving to recover, having lost both his legs. I realised that, although I was in a most dire situation, it could have been so much worse. I know that is a well-worn cliché but it is, nonetheless, true!

That encounter prompted me to get my act together and aim for a full recovery, or at the very least to make the best of the circumstances I now found myself in. Once I had made that choice I found that I had overcome some invisible barrier, like a force field, that had almost sucked me into submission.

As the weeks went by, and surgery was ruled out, my stubborn streak really awakened and I begged to be allowed to go home. The team considered my request and eventually agreed to an early discharge – subject to 'terms & conditions' – the main one being that I would have 24-hour assistance. Well there was only one option that would satisfy that criteria! I was eventually discharged to the care of my parents.

Having lived alone in 'flatland' in the big smoke for five years, the thought of going home to Mam and Dad was daunting and, quite honestly, scared the life out of me.

My homecoming was very emotional. I had made the tough decision to not have my parent's visit me in hospital so we had not seen each other since the night of the accident. I figured my mother would do one of two things. She'd either crumble in a heap of devastation, or adapt an air of stoic strength. Thankfully, she opted for the latter and as I manoeuvred myself and 'Jerome' towards the front door she donned her suit of armour, folded her arms and addressed me by my full title.

'Well, Thomas Joseph Fleming. You certainly outdid yourself this time. I never thought a brass neck could be broken.'

Yes, coming home was the right thing to do. My parents, now my carers, rose to the challenge and all but killed me with kindness. Between overindulgence in good home cooking by day (Mam) and medicinal hot toddies to help me sleep by night (Dad), I ran the risk of becoming an overweight tenor with a fondness for the drink.

I mentioned earlier that I had a stubborn streak, but the overall experience taught me that it's important to know when to ask for, and accept, help. I am forever thankful that I learned that lesson.

Could I have done it without them? Possibly, but certainly not as quickly or as effectively. They provided me with a safety net that I know was vital to my recovery. It wasn't all fairy tale stuff. We clashed on occasion, the novelty of being pampered wore off, and there was something about being back home that threatened my independence. Nothing specific, but enough to fuel my daily fight back to a full recovery, and I worked incredibly hard during that time to allow myself get back to the path I had started to carve. One thing for sure was that from here on in, I'd take no more short cuts.

The medical team had told me I would be out of action for two years. Now two years is a long time for anyone to be *on hold*, and in the music business it's like going back to the first rung of that ladder. Fortunately, I discovered an inner strength, bolstered by the comforting familiar surrounds of home and family, and I fought my way back to a full recovery in less than a year, emerging from that scary and dark period of my life a stronger and better person.

Never ever underestimate your own strength of mind. For me, that car accident – horrific though it was – was a turning point, one which allowed me to dig so deep that I found a part of me that had never been needed up to then.

Yes, I was lucky. Yes, I know not everyone is so lucky, but what I also know, and what I want to share, is that every one of us has within us the ability and the strength to tackle the most adverse situations that life will throw at us.

No, it's not easy. Anything worthwhile rarely is, but I am forever thankful that I gave my recovery my best shot, and to revert to Clifford T. Ward – that cover song on my first solo album – *The Best Is Yet to Come*, well that pretty much says it all.

Be brave, be strong, and believe in yourself – I did, and I am so glad that I did, and for the strength of character that has stayed with me to this day.

Reach for the stars.

Cosmo's

Oliver Sears

Swiss Cottage in Northwest London may have its own underground station, but as far as an identity is concerned, it's something of a curate's egg; a void surrounded by more well-defined areas: Hampstead, home to artists, poets and the Literati to the north with its heath and fresh water swimming ponds, St John's Wood of grand, ambassadorial residences to the west, unfashionable Kilburn to the south, whose border with West Hampstead means that gentrification will inexorably spill over, and the perennially bohemian Camden to the east. A public house in the style of a faux chalet, known as the *Swiss Tavern*, is built on the site of a former tollgate keeper's cottage and gives the area its name.

Today, it's marooned on an island between a dozen lanes of traffic like an incongruous, urban, lighthouse which is connected to the mainland by three sets of pedestrian crossings that bob like marker buoys, measuring progress rather than genuinely offering safe passage. You'll need a drink if you make it across. Behind the pub is a large, red-bricked Odeon cinema, a giant biscuit tin of post-war practicality, and opposite is Camden Library, the largest public library in London, attached to a swimming pool complex; an edifice fabricated with large slats of concrete, interposed with long cathedral-like vitrines, resembling a giant tank track thrown on its side. This is the heart of Swiss Cottage, and it's ugly. No doubt the champions of Brutalism who worship in the high temple of Terminal One at Paris Charles de Gaulle only see *jolie laide*, and have almost certainly proposed this unavoidable landmark to the pantheon of world heritage sites. Be that as it may, Swiss Cottage falls within the triangular shaped post code of NW3. And whether on the foothills that also claim Belsize Park, home to the odd, once well-known, actor, or sweeping up to Hampstead village and its theatre-going burghers, the caviar communists who make sure to fly home from their holiday homes in France to vote Labour, or in an unlikely Alpine-style drinking den, NW3 is the fairy dust that designates boho chic, elevated status and jacked-up property prices.

After the war, Swiss Cottage became home to a small number of Jewish refugees from Eastern Europe, mainly Poland, among them my maternal grandparents, who would often meet in three cafés on either side of a stretch of the Finchley Road, known as Harben Parade. *Louis'* was a smart, Viennese-style pâtisserie with pastries, sweet and savoury, laid out in perfect lines in the window; one of two branches (the other in Hampstead Village) run by its eponymous owner, an émigré from Hungary. Louis drove between the two operations in a powder blue convertible Rolls Royce with a number plate that spelled his name. He needed the reassurance of portable, public opulence to measure his own success and reinforce his self-confidence in his adoptive country; and to remind his patrons what they were paying for.

The *Cosmopolitan*, over the road (known locally as *Cosmo's*) was modest and drab by comparison. It was generally more popular with the refugees who would sit without formality and babble over coffee, an unimaginable luxury during their wartime lives. They also congregated in the *Dorice* which had been open the longest, a smaller café on the same side of the road as *Louis'* but closer to Finchley Road Tube Station. Although they gossiped, squabbled and grumbled about ordinary, everyday gripes like any other group of middle-aged friends, fate had plucked them out, individually, from its own sea of destruction and thrown them into a lifeboat together as a small mercy. All of them had been stripped of everything they knew and loved and understood to be true from their previous existence. Here, in this unassuming corner of London, whose drab lack of personality was its defining character- istic, they attempted to rebuild their broken selves. Laughter was not a common currency of communication between them. They cackled and guffawed but seldom lost themselves in a fit of giggles. Grief had inter- cepted that impulse, but the instinct to love had not abandoned them all. The *Dorice* was referred to as the *Mialem Café*. In English it sounds like the noise a cat makes, but in Polish means, '*I had*'. Here, the refugees reminisced, sometimes out of competitive grief, but very seldom did they articulate the true sum of their losses; 'I had this' and 'I had that' could be measured and noted materially. No one had found the mecha- nism or impulse to calculate the human cost.

New, unlikely marriages were entered into, bonds forged out of the most deeply complex, personal tragedies, and the need to reclaim their identity – the sole reason they had been systematically hunted down; an identity which they defiantly refused to dishonour. New children were made and, for the most part, their former lives were put in lead-lined boxes and never spoken of.

Josek Cukier was a regular at *Cosmo's* where he would meet friends and talk about his life in Swiss Cottage, as he now understood it. Previ- ously, Josek Cukier was a wealthy businessman in Poland. Josek, an affectionate version of Josef and Cukier, pronounced Zucker, the Polish for sugar: Joey Sugar, in English. Josek came from a family of profes- sionals, he was naturally artistic, became a proficient draughtsman and developed an eye for well-crafted objects d'art. In time, he combined this talent with a business acumen and came to own the franchises for Baccarat Crystal and the French cutlery maker Laguiole, in Poland.

The Cukiers had been secular Jews for three generations. They were a well-known and respected family in Krakow, more integrated into Polish gentile society than most Jews, if not entirely assimilated. Josek was a confident, well-adjusted, warm man with few enemies and could be described, in the most traditional sense, as an upstanding member of his community.

Just days before Germany invaded Poland on 1 September 1939, Josek found himself in England on a business trip and when Britain declared war on Germany three days later, he was stranded, unable to return home. He desperately tried to get news of his wife and two young daughters, pressing all available channels – embassies, societies, the Church and the Red Cross – and receiving nothing but silence.

The first few weeks of the war were especially terrifying for those trapped under occupation and unable to escape, as one rule of law swallowed another and chaos, panic and rumour took to the streets.

Whatever information Josek *could* find was fragmentary, contradictory and totally unreliable. He was running through all the possible scenarios, the waves of despair crashing into the constructs of hope and justice he clung to – that they might all be reunited; a dream to drown out the grief of losing his three precious loves and, with them gone, any reason to live. He had exhausted all available lines of enquiry and come up empty handed. He feared that the not knowing, in such heightened circumstances, would devour all sense of decorum, the ability to function, and sanity itself.

But suddenly, as if falling from the sky, he felt the weakest flicker of hope. An acquaintance of a colleague knew someone in the East End of London who was in touch with the Polish Underground. He intimated that, for money, there was a possibility of smuggling out a communication. Josek wrote his letter with such urgency that the words ran into each other. Most of all, he vowed to get them out of Poland and pleaded only that they stay safe and wait for him. He deposited the letter with his colleague along with a payment of ten pounds, an enormous sum in 1939. A month passed without news. Anxiety invaded Josek's organism. Appetite and sleep disappeared like a past tense. His adrenal glands were flooding his system with cortisol, the body's natural response to stress, but overdosing on cortisol only amplified the sensation of anxiety and made him feel permanently nauseous. He had aged ten years. Then, one day his colleague contacted him. He'd received news. Something had come back. And there it was: a letter in his wife's handwriting with two little black and white photographs of his daughters. His hands quivered as he registered the contents, line by line. They were safe. They had moved in with his brother's family. Food was hard to find. The streets were dangerous. Those were the headlines. Josek pored over the two photographs. He was relieved, excited, frightened, and too many things at once. He retreated to his tiny apartment, alone with his precious letter, tantalized and almost entirely depleted. What to do next?

Continuing his search for more information, he received extraordinary news a month later. The British government had arranged for a ship to sail to Gdansk in Northern Poland to rescue stranded British citizens as part of an exchange arrangement brokered with the German authorities. If valid identity papers and places on the boat could be secured, they could be smuggled out to his wife and children and they could all be together again. However, procuring the correct documentation was almost impossible. Ports were blockaded and the immigration authorities were on high alert. Josek had good connections in London and he used them. Within a week he had secured his golden passes. A valid passport for his wife and daughters and three tickets for the voyage back to Southampton – with fifty pounds this time – were given to his contact to send down the same channel of correspondence.

Josek waited. The ship was due in Southampton docks on 2 December 1939. A small cargo of thirty-six British passport holders was expected. Time seemed to lengthen as he counted the days down. The waiting was interminable. Impatience had become his biggest internal enemy. On the scheduled day of arrival, Josek rose early and made his way by train from London to Southampton, clutching a small nosegay of fresh flowers. He waited on the quayside, shivering as the small cruise ship sailed quietly in. He stood together and alone with the rest of the welcoming committee, twenty or so expectant souls who were hoping to begin again with their loved ones; individual worlds that had been torn apart and that now, miraculously were about to be repaired and renewed.

The dock hands tethered the vessel to the quayside, wrapping heavy ropes around thick, black cleats and pulling them taut to a knot. They steadied the landing jetty and prepared for disembarkation. Two minutes passed. Out they filed, clutching children, suitcases and the rest of their lives. Josek could not yet see his family. Still they came. There was a mother with two children, similar in profile to his own wife and daughters, but it wasn't them. A family of six and two elderly women, probably sisters. And then there were no more. Josek froze. He then started to tremble and, in panic, mingled between the new arrivals, convinced that in giddy anticipation he must have missed them coming ashore. But he could not find them. He spoke to one of the personnel on board who asked him to wait while he fetched someone with the passenger manifest. Another man in a peaked hat, wielding a clip board, approached. He slid his finger down the list, typed alphabetically.

'Yes', he said, 'Esther, Myriam and Anja Cukier. They were onboard but everyone has disembarked.'

'Impossible', replied Josek, 'I watched everyone step off and they weren't there.'

'I'm sorry Sir but there are no passengers left aboard.'

Josek spent the next hour walking around the port of Southampton looking for his wife and children. He could not understand how they had managed to leave the ship without him seeing them, or they him. It was inexplicable. There was no one else to ask. Where on earth were they? They were on the list. It took him until the evening for the full horror of what had just unfolded to sink in. The woman with the two girls who vaguely resembled his wife and daughters must have travelled using his wife and daughters' documentation. His family had been duped out of them or the documents had been stolen and sold on. Or they had been murdered for them. Or the precious paperwork had been intercepted and simply never reached them. There were many scenarios that Josek constructed and played out in his mind. All he ever knew was that as he waited for them to come to him, the wrong three individuals stepped ashore. Someone else's luck had robbed him of his beloved family. Unwittingly, he had given to three complete strangers not just the chance of a new life but of life itself. Three strangers who had folded into the crowd, to be welcomed by another husband or father, no less desperate than himself, and who may have known nothing of the circum-stances that gave them false documents, new names and perhaps their only chance of escape. And, worse still, had Josek's actions condemned his loved ones to death? Was he to suffer the personal ignominy and humiliation of having paid for their fate, financially? Who deserves that kind of unnatural cruelty?

Josek never had another communication from any member of his family again. He did not utter a word to another living soul for a year. It was not a self-imposed vow of silence. He just couldn't find or form the words. A few years after the war he married again. Blanka was also a survivor; a warm, undemanding woman who did what she could to insulate Josek from his trauma. They did not have any more children. My mother, Monika who had herself survived the Holocaust as a young child, told me that his apartment was bedecked with sketches he made of his daughters, made from those two precious photographs that he had received, the only images he had of them beyond those he kept in the privacy of his memory.

She asked him if he had drawn pictures of anything else.

He replied, 'What else is there to draw?'

THE HOLY MOUNTAIN

Tommy Marren

Since I was knee-high to a grasshopper I always had a fascination with, and a wish to, work in broadcasting. My early memories were of sunny Sundays listening to Radio Éireann and wondering how the maestro that was GAA commentator Michael O'Hehir could always sound so enthusiastic – even when the game was one-sided! I also vividly recall watching the Dublin Horse Show and re-running what I had just watched by setting up my own concocted man-made fences (cardboard boxes and galvanised sheets in the back garden) and pretending to be horse, rider and commentator all in one!

As things turned out I did become a radio broadcaster, and for over thirty years have been working with Midwest Radio, the local station for Mayo. I can honestly say that I have a wonderful job that offers variety, opportunity and, above all, the chance to meet incredible people from all walks of life. I've covered many sensitive, and sometimes scary, subjects, including landslides, general elections, murders, a Papal visit and, of course, the emergence of a Mayo Taoiseach.

Compiled by BRENDAN POWER

I've also had the privilege of interviewing many people who have encountered all sorts of challenges in their lives. Each one is unique but I am always in awe of the bravery and courage of people who are facing medical battles where the odds are heavily stacked against them. One such person is Charlie Bird – a household name in Ireland for over four decades. As I write this, I have to declare that I've never met Charlie personally but, like so many others, I feel I have known him all my life. As RTÉ's chief Crime Correspondent he was synonymous in getting to the heart of a breaking story, following it through to the end and delivering accurate and forensic reporting. He has always been one of the most inspiring journalists to grace the airwaves in Ireland.

When news filtered through that Charlie had been diagnosed with Motor Neurone Disease in late 2021 there was a genuine air of sadness across the country. It seemed unfair that someone who had devoted his entire life to public service broadcasting was now himself the centre of attention. His honesty about what was unfolding before him was simply incredible. I know that Charlie isn't the first, and most definitely won't be the last, to be diagnosed with this awful condition. Many others have faced similar challenges but because Charlie has been in the public eye for so long this was a body-blow for all of us who admire him so much.

It would have been understandable if Charlie had chosen to deal with his challenge privately. No media hype or fuss. However, he chose to deal with his illness in a different way. He spoke openly about his fear of the future, the unknowns around how long it would be before he lost his voice or would become immobile. He was sincere when he spoke about the plethora of emotions he was going through and his fear of how or when it will all end.

When Charlie openly declared his wish to climb Croagh Patrick on an RTÉ *Late Late Show* appearance, in the lead up to Christmas 2021, I immediately thought that this was an opportunity for me to help. After all, Midwest Radio is the local radio station for Mayo and the holy mountain is on our doorstep. It was a no brainer. We had the platform to help Charlie and I immediately set the wheels in motion to promote the 'Climb with Charlie' challenge, and to inspire our listeners to become part of what turned out to be an event that brought people together in all corners of the world.

The date for the climb was set for Saturday, 2 April 2021. I emailed Charlie offering our assistance and got an immediate response. Subsequently, Charlie joined me on air to talk about his wish and the avalanche of goodwill we got from listeners was mind blowing. It was one of those interviews where you just knew everybody was behind the man, and a tsunami of support ensued. Everybody wanted to help – it was like it was payback time for Charlie. On the morning of his radio interview with me he casually mentioned how amazing it would be if the climb could be live-streamed so that people could watch his progress every step of the way, no matter where they were in the world. It was one wish that was easier said than done. No electricity on the mountain, poor internet coverage and tricky underfoot conditions were the immediate obstacles to a possible live stream.

Following the radio interview, I gathered the programming and technical team together and it was decided that we would pull out all the stops – if it were technically possible to do a live stream, then Midwest Radio would be the one to do it. We gathered the technology, did the relevant testing, agreed that a live stream was possible, and duly committed to doing it.

In the weeks prior to the walk it became evident that Charlie's health was deteriorating. His speech was becoming indistinct and there was a feeling that perhaps he may not be able to climb the iconic mountain. But in true Charlie Bird style, he rallied. A special device was developed whereby Charlie could continue to communicate. He knew what he wanted to say and by the wonders of modern technology, so did we.

The days leading up to the climb were frantic. The number of things that could go wrong clearly outnumbered the things that could go right – even down to how we were going to transport diesel to the top of the mountain to keep the generators going! Two men came to the rescue and agreed to carry it up in five-gallon drums – another problem solved! The technical equipment was air-lifted on the day before the climb and in the true spirit of how wishes can come true, things started falling into place. Logistically this was our biggest ever technical challenge but I had a sense that the gods were on our side – and fortunately they were!

Our broadcast started at 7.00 a.m. on that Saturday morning. I was the main studio anchor and our team were on site at Croagh Patrick an hour earlier. As I arrived at the studio in Ballyhaunis it was raining – the first rain we'd seen in weeks and I wished that it might just stop for one more day! When I spoke to my colleagues on site at the mountain they said that weather conditions there were perfect. In fact, a steady stream of walkers were already making their way up the mountain.

Just after 10.00 a.m. Charlie arrived, and the walk commenced. Alongside his devoted wife, Claire, and a host of celebrities, Charlie began his pilgrimage, and we were with him every step of the way. There were a few minor technical hitches along the way but our team delivered in spades. We captured the live scenes of the climb and our social media channels went crazy as millions of people around the world watched the walk unfold live before their eyes. Those on the mountain offered their support with banners and flags and within two hours Charlie had reached the summit. The Clew Bay Pipe Band were on hand to escort him to the chapel where he lit a series of candles. He cried. He embraced those around him. He clenched his fist numerous times to bystanders as if to say 'I did it'. He cried some more – so too did the rest of us.

Over three million euro was raised for Pieta House and the Motor Neurone Disease Association as people walked local hills, mountains and stairs in every corner of the world. One man's wish became a worldwide phenomenon.

For most of us it is unimaginable to face a challenge like that. To have the capacity to be so willing and courageous at such a difficult time takes immense inner strength. The song 'One Day at a Time' comes to mind:

'Show me the stairway, I have to climb,
Lord for my sake, teach me to take
One day at a time.'

To be part of granting him his wish will be one of the most treasured memories of my broadcasting career.

Charlie continues to take it 'One Day at a Time'.

What Is Success?

John Magnier

I believe success is doing what you want to do in life, and for me that is being able to make my living working with horses. Since childhood, horses have not just been an important part of my life, but have always been, and still are, my passion.

Your interests and your passion will be different to mine, but whatever it is, when you love what you do, you can't wait to get out of bed in the morning and get started. Work will never be a chore; no matter how difficult it is, no matter how many problems you run into along the way, it will always be a pleasure if you are following your passion.

I left school when I was fifteen. Not through choice, but because my father died of cancer and, as the eldest of four children, it was up to me to help my mother in the running of our family farm and stud.

Losing a parent when you are young hurts badly, but it does impart one very important lesson that I quickly understood: never take the gift of life for granted. Your life and your health are precious gifts to be valued above all else, and that applies not just to you, but also to those you love and care for.

Shortly before he died, my father reminded me of the importance of being sensitive to the feelings of others: work colleagues, friends and neighbours, the widow who has lost her husband, the family who have fallen on hard times. When you meet someone in that situation, don't turn away if you can help in any way.

From time to time, life tests us all. We all endure misfortune, we all make mistakes, sometimes we think we know it all and at other times we wonder if we know anything. The truth is that nobody knows it all, everybody fails in one way or another, at some time or another. Don't be despondent when that happens, it's a part of life that reminds us, in simple terms, that we are all human, and consequently it is important that we always keep some perspective.

Never be afraid to ask questions if you don't understand something. Even when something is explained to you and you still don't *get it*, ask again. Perhaps you might feel foolish for asking again, but the really foolish thing to do would be not to ask. I know this from experience; I never fully understood the dot.com bubble and I was too proud to ask anyone to explain it to me. It was a very expensive mistake and one that you shouldn't make.

When God created us, he gave us one mouth and two ears. When you use them in those proportions – listening twice as much as you speak – you will learn a great deal.

In business, and in life, what goes around comes around. Success or failure in your chosen profession will not determine the quality of your life. That will be determined by the way you treat those who are closest to you, your family and friends.

Look after those you love, they are very special people.

An Unlikely Hero

David Carroll

In the middle of March 1911, the southern coast of Ireland was being pounded by high winds and raging seas. In Waterford they referred to it as the worst storm for sixteen years, similar to the time the *Moresby*, en route from Cardiff to South America, had been wrecked in Dungarvan Bay with the loss of eighteen lives, including the captain's wife and two children.

It looked as though history might repeat itself on Saturday, 18 March when the schooner *Teaser*, en route from Swansea to Dingle Bay, got into difficulties in the storm and was driven on to the Black Rocks off Curragh Strand, close to Ardmore, from where the coast guards set out with their rocket apparatus to go to the vessel's assistance. In poor visibility they fired their rockets with lines attached and, with great skill, landed them on the deck of the *Teaser*. The three-man crew, exhausted and suffering from exposure, were so numbed by the cold, however, that they were unable to make use of the lifelines.

Ignoring the danger, and putting their own lives at risk, two of the coast guards – Richard Barry and Alexander Neal – plunged into the icy waters and started swimming towards the vessel, which was aground about a quarter of a mile offshore. From the outset it was clear they had set themselves an impossible task and so it proved as they were beaten back by the heavy seas, into the arms of their waiting colleagues who hauled them back on to the beach.

Stationed at Helvick Head, the nearest lifeboat was the *James Stevens 16* (one of twenty lifeboats built with a legacy of almost seven million pounds, in 2022 terms, left by timber merchant James Stevens of Birmingham). Although efforts were made to alert the crew by telephone, communications failed – probably due to the lines being blown down – so a messenger had to be sent by road. The lifeboat was launched at eight o'clock and made its way under sail. With fifteen men on board, and with the coxswain displaying exceptional seamanship in the teeth of the storm, it took them two-and-a-half hours to reach the Curragh, by which time all that could be done had been done.

As news of the wreck spread, a large crowd gathered on shore and from its midst, 40-year-old Fr John O'Shea, the mild-mannered curate at St Declan's Church, stepped forward, called for volunteers, and set out on foot for Ardmore where he knew there was a fisherman's boat. His team of volunteers was said to number close to one hundred and together they pushed and pulled the heavy boat over a mile of rough ground and then manhandled it down on to the beach. Without a moment's hesitation, the priest put on a lifebelt and called to the crowd for a crew. To get into an open boat in such appalling weather would be seen by most people as sheer madness, but on that day there was no shortage of volunteers. Seven men were chosen, including a police constable and the two coast guards who had earlier attempted to swim to the schooner. As soon as they were on board, others from the crowd pushed the boat into the crashing waves.

Their chances of success were almost non-existent, but against all odds they eluded the deadly rocks, escaped being swamped by the huge seas, and avoided being crushed against the side of the *Teaser*, which had been listing heavily to starboard and was now on her beam ends with sails flapping dangerously in the gale. Incredibly, the priest, police constable Daniel Lawton, the two coast guards and hotelier William Harris somehow managed to board the stricken vessel, placing themselves at even greater risk of injury, or worse.

To avoid being thrown into the sea when the ship grounded, the crew had lashed themselves to the rigging but, tragically, for two of them the rescuers arrived too late, they were beyond all aid. As the men from Ardmore fought to release them from the rigging, one of the crew slid across the deck and into the sea. Without hesitation, coast guards Barry and Neal jumped in after him and in spite of the mountainous waves, managed to get him back on board. Coast guard Barry was now so exhausted that he had to be hauled from the sea by Constable Lawton and immediately collapsed on the deck prompting Fr O'Shea to administer the last rites, which, fortunately, proved to be redundant.

They succeeded in getting the crew onto the fishing boat and once again fought their way through the waves and foaming surf to bring them ashore where they were taken to the shelter of a neighbouring house. Despite everything possible being done for him by Dr Tim Foley, whose surgery was on Parson's Hill in Ardmore, the third crew member was pronounced dead soon afterwards. Father O'Shea had done all he could to save them, but sadly his best efforts, and those of his colleagues, were to no avail and all that was left now was for him to administer the last rites.

For his gallantry, Father O'Shea, was awarded the RNLI's highest award, the Gold Medal, which, two months later, was presented to him in Dublin by Lord Aberdeen, the Lord Lieutenant of Ireland. A few weeks earlier he had accompanied his volunteer crew to Buckingham Palace where King George V presented them with the Silver Sea Gallantry Medal awarded by the Board of Trade. The Carnegie Hero Fund Trust also presented him with a gold watch, their highest award.

The good father was to the fore again less than two years later when the *Maréchal de Noailles*, a French barque en route from Glasgow to the French penal colony of New Caledonia in the South Pacific, was blown ashore at Mine Head, not far from Ardmore. On this occasion Father O'Shea was part of the coast guard rocket apparatus team, which also included his former crew mates Richard Barry and Alexander Neal. With the road being too rough for the rocket wagon, the crew carried the unwieldly apparatus fourteen miles on foot, arriving at the scene of the wreck at two o'clock in the morning. Ignoring their own exhaustion, they immediately set to work and within hours had brought the entire crew of the barque safely to shore using a breeches buoy.

In 1924, by which time he was parish priest in Carrick-on-Suir, he was again honoured for his bravery with the award of the Empire Gallantry Medal. There were seven other recipients who, together with the priest made up the only eight surviving Gold Medal holders, from the 109 awarded in the first hundred years of the institution. In the lavish surroundings of London's Cecil Hotel, the awards were presented at the RNLI centenary dinner by the Prince of Wales, who expressed his disappointment that Fr O'Shea was unable to attend due to illness.

The Empire Gallantry Medal was replaced by the George Cross in 1940, and the following year he was invited by the King to attend an investiture in Buckingham Palace where he received his George Cross, the highest civilian award bestowed by the British government, and equal in stature to the Victoria Cross, the highest military award for gallantry.

Reverend Father John Michael O'Shea GC, an unlikely hero, passed away peacefully on 19 September 1942, at the age of seventy-one, and was laid to his eternal rest behind the Cross of Calvary in the grounds of the Church of the Assumption in Ballyporeen, Co Tipperary, where, as parish priest, he had ended his vocation.

BECOMING OURSELVES

Jennifer Horgan

'O chestnut tree, great rooted blossomer,
Are you the leaf, the blossom or the bole?
O body swayed to music, O brightening glance,
How can we know the dancer from the dance?'
WB Yeats

At some point in the night, my six-year-old daughter makes her way into my bed. I wake to find her curled up beside me. In the half-light, she looks like she did as a newborn. Her mouth is open, her chin raised. Her hair smells like maple syrup. I breathe it in, a quiet moment before the alarm goes.

I wake the other two. My husband flicks the kettle, starts to pack lunches. The kitchen feels too bright, glaring against the dripping, ink-black window. I gather toothbrushes, hairbrushes, bags, coats, schoolbooks, pencil cases – send them on their way.

Each of my children has their way of navigating our morning routine. The eldest gets everything done quickly. He practically dresses in bed, then finds a quiet corner to read or watch TV. My middle child dresses slowly, rummaging through every wardrobe in the house, clothes bombs exploding behind her. My youngest fights to wear the same scraggy top every day, which is why it's often drying on a radiator as she eats her cereal.

My students are the same – in their tendency and desire to do things their way. As a teacher I try to give them as much freedom as I can, but the system works against me all the time.

I have an American pen-pal who teaches me a lot. He likes to muse on big questions like why we writers write in the first place. We exchange poetry. He thinks it's to remind ourselves that we're here, little collections of stardust, fleeting, but here, nonetheless. He thinks we write to make our mark. Even if my students don't enjoy my subject, I want them to know something about this way of thinking. I want them to zoom out of the here and now a little, enough to be able to see it happening. He also tells me that each one of us has more atoms than there are stars in the night sky and that all the conscious and unconscious thoughts we have exceed the number of lives of the entire past. Each one of us is a multitude. His way of thinking reminds me of the Yeats poem, about the dancer and the dance. The idea as I understand it, that we're in constant motion, an ongoing act of becoming. We are what we do. Or at least we should be.

When I arrive in class, Sixth-year English, Simon is already there. He's always appropriately dressed for the weather. This morning, I discard my battered umbrella by the secretary's office, wipe myself down. Meanwhile, Simon carefully removes his full-length wet gear and takes the lid off his thermos to sip his tea. I wonder will my youngest be the same at his age. She's recently started to design robotic fish. Every part has a function. It's probably why she wears the same top every day. Why change one top if it's doing its job? Functionality is everything.

Simon doesn't like English literature, but he needs a high grade to progress in our current system. He goes through the motions when he writes essays. He struggles to answer the question clearly. He struggles to memorise quotations.

Sarah arrives next. She's all heart and soul – her empathy muscles are almost too developed; she's muscle bound in her anxiety. She says project work and continuous assessment would help her. She tells me she stays up reading all night. If I were her age, I'd want her to be my friend. She's endlessly cool and human. I worry that her skin is too thin though. She mentions her boyfriend a lot. I find myself hoping he's as young and as good as she is.

We say the Leaving Cert is fair because it's anonymous, but that anonymity masks neglect. One in four learners has an additional need in Ireland. Schools are under-funded as are child mental health services. Anonymity in the exam means everyone is treated the same. But they're not the same and they're not given the same chances. It might be hard for us to fix every societal injustice but what we can do is let students go their own way, enter their own process of becoming. Our system should work for them, not against them. For some students, school is a dead-end, a cul de sac. They simply get through the days. If they are in a school without the Leaving Cert Applied (most schools) but have no aptitude for their core, compulsory subjects, their days are long, and often come without reward or recognition. They are made to feel like a square block, knocking against a round hole. They just won't fit.

I wish the purpose of education in Ireland was to give students the space and freedom to become themselves. I'd like our schools to offer a range of subjects up to the age of sixteen or so. I'd like these subjects to be taught by brilliant, empowered, and trusted teachers who'd work collaboratively in a supportive environment. I'd like subject choices to be non-gendered, fully resourced. And I'd like space for the student in the final two years of study, to carve their own paths without compulsory subjects, without burdens and barriers stacked against them.

I'd like our system to treat each of my children, my students, and my colleagues kindly.

An artist I once met announced confidently that we're entering a Renaissance. I like that idea. I like to think that history will remember us, and this time, as something special. This artist believes that we should celebrate our individual identities if we want to get back to our universal and shared roots. I like that idea too. It reminds me of the stardust my pen-pal talks about. I like to think that we are all unique collections of that one thing, and that one thing is our humanity.

So, whether it makes sense or not, I'd like the purpose of education to capture the stardust, the golden syrup, the dancers, and the dance. I'd like it to have something to do with giving us all space and freedom and encouragement.

Education should let us get joyfully lost in the experience of that blossoming, that endlessly messy process of becoming ourselves.

GOLD

Jason Smyth

My parents began to notice that something was not right with my vision when I was just eight-years-old. They noticed me starting to move closer and closer to the television in order to watch it, and saw that, instead of looking directly at them, I would look into the distance when I was talking to them. I was also finding it more and more difficult to see the writing on my school text books.

A trip to the optician was arranged, and quickly followed by a couple of visits to the hospital where I was examined by a specialist who informed me I had an eye condition called Stargardt Disease. As an eight-year-old boy I had no idea what that meant, but in very simple terms it was explained to me that my central vision had started to disappear and this was why things were getting more and more blurry. I now had less than 10 percent of my vision.

What did that mean for my future?

Was my vision going to stabilise or continue to get worse? Well, it seems that was an unknown as it was different for each person.

Could I be completely blind at some point? Yes.

Were there any cures out there? Unfortunately not.

The stark reality is that our vision impacts all aspects of our life. From socialising and interacting with people to having independence. From career paths to everyday experiences. Imagine for a moment going about life with your eyes closed. How much different would things be? Although that's not completely accurate as I have a small bit of vision, I'm sure you understand my point, and why I felt the road ahead did not seem as bright as it had, nor like one that had plenty of opportunities.

My default position in that situation, like so many others facing difficult moments in life, was to look at the negatives, look at all the things I would miss out on, the things that would make my life so much more challenging, and even at times asked myself the question – 'Why me?' Was this fair? What did I do to deserve to be in this position? It was definitely not the place I wanted to be in mentally. I struggled to accept the situation I was in and, as a result, it put a big dent in both my confidence, and my belief in myself.

Fast forward to today, over 25 years later, and it is interesting to compare the difference in perspectives. From looking forward many years ago, filled with doubts and unknowns, to today, looking backwards on an incredible journey with so many opportunities. I have experienced unforgettable moments, enjoyed unbelievable highs, had a lot of satisfaction and joy in pushing the boundaries of what is possible through my sporting career this far and, hopefully, I have inspired a few people on the way. I have a career that has had me competing internationally for the last 19 years, one that has had me standing on top of many podiums throughout the world to receive medals and hear the national anthem played in my honour. One that's had me competing at four Paralympic Games, winning six gold medals, and, in total, 21 gold medals at international championships. I have broken world records, never been beaten at any major championship and have been described as the fastest Paralympian of all time. I have been in some of the best performance environments and learned the art of success, which has helped me knock down barriers. I have had the opportunity to meet and learn from all sorts of different people, and experience their cultures in many different places throughout the world.

It's impossible to describe fully the positive impact my journey has had on me but what I find interesting is that it would not have happened unless I was diagnosed with an eye disease. That was what led me to being a Paralympic athlete and, from there, the experiences that came with my success. The thing that gave me so many doubts, knocked me back so many times and brought a lot of uncertainty was the same thing that eventually brought me incredible opportunities, and turned into one of my greatest strengths.

So, what has my journey taught me? Well, my experiences have taught me that the difficult moments I find myself in, no matter how difficult they seem, are less important than what I am going to do about them, how I act and react to what's happened. It's not about how many times I get knocked down but how many times I keep getting back up and pushing beyond where I was. In sport we talk about *controlling the controllables*. In other words, spend your time and energy influencing the things that you can influence and forget about the things you can't. Focusing on that allowed me to start moving forward, to be honest with myself, and accept where I was. It started to shift the way I looked at what was in front of me. It started to help me look for the opportunities in each situation, especially the difficult situations.

Improvement and progression, in my experience, comes best when I am forced out of my comfort zone, have to work hard at finding solutions, be pushed in ways I haven't been before, which often helps in the refining process. So, it's through challenges I have the opportunity to improve and progress the most. Shouldn't I then embrace the challenges I face? In fact, doesn't that mean the greater the challenge, the greater the opportunity to progress? What followed that was belief, belief in myself and what I could overcome as well as achieve. That led me to hope as I looked forward and considered the possibilities.

The most powerful thing we all have is our mind. It drives what we do or don't do. In my journey that's one of the most impactful things I've discovered, the ability I have to achieve more than I ever thought was possible. The right mindset gave me the chance to unlock a bit more of my potential. The best part about it is everyone has the ability to do the same thing: unlock a bit more of their potential by shifting their mindset.

Rory Staunton: Saving Lives Every Day

Niall O'Dowd

Sixteen thousand lives, including those of many children, have been saved by an Irish family who refuse to accept their son's tragic death has been in vain.

In 2012 Rory Staunton, Queen's, New York, son of Mayo-born Ciaran Staunton and Orlaith O'Dowd from Louth, was just a few weeks short of his thirteenth birthday when he died from a deadly, but all too common, disease known as sepsis. Thanks to his parents, however, from that terrible tragedy came triumph, and thousands of saved lives.

Rory was a lively, super smart kid who was already involving himself in environmental and political issues, already a champion debater, even writing to North Korean dictator Kim Jong-un asking why he was treating his own people so badly. Rory always sided with the underdog and was known to protect younger kids from bullying. In school he championed a campaign to end the use of the word 'retarded' to describe people, and to use terms like 'special needs' instead.

Towering above the majority of his peers, at five foot ten, and with a shock of red hair, he made quite an impression wherever he went. He was intensely proud of his Irish heritage and Saint Patrick's Day was his favourite. Rory also retained his love for Mayo's football team and had supported the green and red in Croke Park with his father on two memorable occasions. This love of sports, which was evident to all, made his premature death even tougher to handle.

During a school basketball game in Queens he fell and cut his elbow. Initially it appeared to be a fairly innocuous wound, but it was not cleaned properly and, incredibly, a few days later Rory was dead from a blood infection known as sepsis, a disease which is normally evidenced by one or more of these symptoms:

- Rapid breathing and heart rate
- Shortness of breath
- Confusion or disorientation
- Extreme pain or discomfort
- Fever and shivering
- Clammy or sweaty skin

Rory died after his condition was missed by attending physicians when he was brought to the hospital. Following his death, the impact was such that his story was featured on the homepage of the *New York Times*, the *Today Show* on NBC and *People* magazine, to mention just a few outlets, all asking the same question: 'How could this happen?'

His parents determined that their best way to honour Rory was to ensure that no other children, or adults, would die due to the lack of sepsis knowledge, even by medical professionals. Their amazing work has resulted in numerous lives in New York State being saved by the Rory Protocols. These are a set of basic guidelines put in place to ensure no one will die unnecessarily, due to ignorance of the condition, which can often be cured by antibiotics if caught in time.

In April 2017, their success made the *New York Times* home page again, and since that article appeared thousands more have been saved.

In a report, the New York State Department of Health pointed out that sepsis develops in response to infection, and can lead to tissue damage, organ failure, and death. It is the leading cause of in-hospital deaths in the United States and although more than 1.7 million Americans are diagnosed with sepsis annually, many other cases are missed. They estimate that the establishment of mandatory sepsis protocols in all New York State hospitals was responsible for saving more than 16,000 lives in the four-year period between 2015 and 2019.

Rory and his foundation, now known as 'End Sepsis', are ensuring that doctors and nurses all over America, and eventually the world, will ask that profound question: 'Could it be sepsis?', when examining a patient who has a high fever and no obvious cause of illness.

The protocols are now set in stone and since the enactment of Rory's Regulations, hospitals are now required to adopt important protocols that help with the early detection and treatment of the disease. When New York State Health Commissioner Dr Mary T. Bassett told a group that sepsis is a serious and potentially life-threatening medical condition, and explained how it is caused by a reaction throughout a person's body in response to an infection, she also confirmed that these protocols have played an important role in saving thousands of New Yorkers' lives.

Ciaran and Orlaith Staunton are certain Rory would be a happy, thriving 24-year-old if Rory's Regulations had been enforced back in 2012. 'No family should have to live with the pain of losing a child,' they say. 'But in Rory's case we can try to ensure other families do not go through what we had to.'

Pilot hero Sully Sullenberger, who saved 155 lives when he landed his plane in the Hudson River, considers Rory one of his heroes. He has campaigned for airline-type take-off checklists to be used in hospitals and is quoted as saying that, 'Rory was on track to do great things, but his life was cut short by a preventable chain of medical errors that kept his doctors from recognizing the symptoms of a deadly infection that began after he scraped his arm in the school gym.'

Rory's foundation receives hundreds of letters every year from grateful parents who believe Rory's Regulations saved their children's lives. One mother wrote about how her daughter's earache and temperature was being dismissed until she insisted that sepsis be looked at as a possible cause. Another mother was turned away from several hospitals because she was so insistent on a sepsis test, which was indeed her child's true problem.

Although 16,000 sounds like a huge number to save, it is only the tip of the iceberg. Ciaran and Orlaith Staunton have now embarked on the next phase, making sure a new federal set of Rory's Regulations spreads nationwide to save thousands more lives.

Both Orlaith and Ciaran firmly believe Rory is with them every step of the way and say that without Rory's spirit and presence they would never be able to carry on. They are confident that someday Rory's Regulations will spread even further and help save kids, and adults, with sepsis all over the world from Africa to the Arctic.

Not bad for a little boy who just wanted to be remembered for doing good.

He did far better than that.

He did great.

No More Cruise Control

Phillip Khan-Panni

It began with a high-speed car crash.

It was a warm, sunny Sunday afternoon and I was on my way to Stansted airport with my then girlfriend, Evelyn. We were a little tight for time, having made a brief diversion to wish my brother a happy birthday.

The M11 was packed. I was in the fast lane, my red Nissan sports car hemmed in by heavy traffic. Evelyn was asleep beside me and I was tired too. You know those tiny moments when you nod off and shake yourself awake? I had a series of those, each lasting only a fraction of a second, but it was worrying. I wanted to pull over and rest on the hard shoulder, but there was no gap to allow me to change lanes.

Suddenly I was gone. Asleep at the wheel, in the fast lane of the M11, approaching a right-hand bend. Somehow, I drifted across three lanes of speeding traffic without hitting anything. As I came off the motorway, the bumping woke Evelyn. She screamed. That woke me and, still half asleep, I could see I was about fifteen or eighteen feet from a hard head-on crash.

The mind works incredibly fast in a crisis. In a millisecond (still travelling at about 70 mph) I considered taking the crash, but visualised Evelyn injured and bleeding and decided I didn't want her hurt. Later I realised what an important moment that had been. So, I took corrective action.

Whipping the wheel clockwise, I managed to change the car's direction of travel. It aquaplaned over the tall grass, giving me no control, skidded across the hard shoulder and crashed sideways into a passing lorry. In a high-speed crash you are aware of many things. I knew that if I struck the bar between the front and rear axles it would slice off the top half of my car and our heads with it. Instead, we struck the twin rear wheels of the lorry, bounced off and spun, ending up backwards in a ditch. There was glass everywhere and the car was a write-off.

Evelyn and I climbed out of the wreck unhurt, but rather shaken up. The lorry had stopped along the road and the driver walked back to see if we were all right. I apologised for causing him the delay and called the AA. The police turned up unbidden, having seen the crash on the motorway camera. The policeman was friendly and courteous, going through the necessary breathalyser routine. He told me the incident would be considered for further action, but he doubted there would be any.

We missed the flight, of course, and during the long delay before the AA could collect the car (and us) I became very cold and began to shiver. It might have been shock. Evelyn was rather subdued. But we returned to base and, as she put it, we looked after each other. There was a strong bonding.

Two very significant events followed directly from that crash.

The first was a realisation that changed the direction of my life. The second was an event that ensured I would have a life of any kind.

In reverse order, I told my GP about the car crash and that I'd been falling asleep at my desk. Not only that, as a professional speaker, singer and runner I had noticed some breathlessness. He referred me to a cardiologist and gave me a letter, which I lost. I did not understand why I should see a heart man, but the breathlessness continued and when I came across the referral letter again, I made an appointment.

The cardiologist put me on a treadmill test, telling me the average time was nine minutes. Despite being a runner, I came off at seven minutes. Recognising that there was a problem, he arranged to do an angiogram. That involved sticking a needle in the artery in my groin, injecting a dye and marking its flow.

'What have you found?' I asked when it was over.

'You are going to need a double heart bypass,' he said, without preamble. 'Next Wednesday, and don't fly.' He told me one of my main cardiac arteries was 95 percent blocked, another 70 percent locked. I'd been running (literally) on very little oxygen. Marathons, cross-country and more.

'Is there some alternative?' I wanted to know, thinking of stents.

'Yes,' he replied, 'A massive, disabling heart attack.'

'I'll take the surgery,' I said. But I requested a one-week delay to allow me to complete a book I had just started writing.

Throughout all of this I had not paused to consider any of the conse-quences, and for the next few days I was focused simply on completing my book, *Stand & Deliver: Leave Them Stirred Not Shaken*. Some of the early chapters I had started on a PC but was now switching to a Mac. The two machines were on different floors in my Bromley townhouse and I was having difficulty getting them to speak to each other. I had to copy a file to a disk and carry it to the other computer on another floor, then download and translate it as necessary.

On the very day I went into hospital for my bypass I was running up and down the stairs, transferring files from one computer to the other, linking them all in a single file for the printer. It was a day of huge stress, during which I was risking a heart attack. Evelyn and my son were watching me at work and wondering if they would get any lunch. Job done with less than an hour to spare, we took off for London Bridge Hospital.

The next day the surgeon got out his Black & Decker and opened me up. Five hours later I was in ICU talking nonsense about beer to my visiting family. Six days later I was back at home, gingerly walking up and down the stairs and down the road with a cushion held against my chest. My sternum was being held together by what looked like paper clips. A ten-inch scar still adorns my chest.

In a way, that event marked a turning point. For some years I'd been a widower with my life on cruise control. I was lucky to have a partner, Evelyn, who was just there, providing such support as I might need. But it was not fair to expect her to fill an empty space without proper recognition. And it was the flash of insight in the car crash, when I knew I didn't want her hurt, that I properly understood her importance to me. That was the realisation I mentioned earlier.

Many a widower settles into a new relationship with a touch of reluctance to replace the wife who died, and I've heard people speak of their 'Dad and his partner'. A kind of unresolved relationship. So, who was Evelyn to me? I asked myself. Not just a convenient companion. It was plain that she was entitled to her own status in my life. We decided to get married. Not immediately, but once we made the decision, we acted fast.

Venue? We chose Trinity College, Dublin, where Evelyn had taken one of her degrees. As luck would have it, they had a vacant slot on a Saturday morning four months later. Reception? We found La Stampa in Dawson Street, with its magnificent dining room that would require no decoration. The manager was a young Frenchman who was keen to have a lunchtime wedding party on a Saturday. We worked out a great deal, and he offered us the Samsara Mezzanine next door to continue after 4.30 p.m. (We partied till after midnight.)

We were lucky with the photographer, the wedding cake, the bubbly and music for the reception. The total budget would astonish anyone who asked. For the wedding ceremony itself we were also very fortunate. The celebrant was a Canadian Jesuit priest who had been my class teacher in the Himalayan town of Darjeeling. He flew over especially to marry us. We planned a musical service with the help of a nun who brought her choir, the New Life Singers of Darndale – a cluster of youths with the voices of angels.

Ninety people came. My son was best man and I had family and friends from England and further afield. It was an incredible occasion, followed by the reception that continued until well after midnight. In a sense it reinforced my connection with Ireland. In the fullness of time, I decided to retire to Ireland and by chance we settled in a house almost within sight of Evelyn's granny's house in Naas.

What was the significance of this series of events? What was the snail trail from that car crash on the M11?

In truth, it began some years before, when my first wife died tragically and unexpectedly. It caused me two lasting effects – first, I was deeply traumatised, and secondly, I became indecisive. With the help of a brilliant counsellor I was able to resume a way of being similar to the way I had been. But I was on cruise control, drifting along, fitting in as best I could. It wasn't fair on my children, and it wasn't fair on my new partner, Evelyn.

I've heard many a speech or presentation about some person's triumph over adversity and thought, 'I don't have that kind of story to tell'. When you are in the middle of a battle to stay on your feet, repeated knockdowns feel like the norm. You tell yourself, 'This is the way it is. Don't complain, don't tell others what you are going through. Just manage.'

That came home to me rather forcibly soon after June died. I was at the bar in my running club, Blackheath Harriers, when a man I knew quite well asked me how I was doing (i.e. coping with my wife's death). I replied, 'I have some good days and some bad ones.' A week later, a mutual friend told me she had met that Harrier at a dinner party and he had told her about our passing encounter, adding, 'I was really embarrassed.' Clearly, he had embellished what I'd said and was dining out on it.

It took the car crash to jolt me into taking charge of my life again, to stop accepting that this was the way it was going to stay. It faced me in a different direction, re-aligned my sense of purpose, and enabled me to see the good in what I already have. When friends comment on my garden and point out the dandelions and weeds, I see only the visiting bees.

But at least I'm no longer travelling in cruise control.

From the Top Down

Amy Molloy

I've cried at the top of the Eiffel Tower and crawled along the walls of the Empire State Building with my eyes shut – but neither experience came close to abseiling down an eight-storey building in Dublin.

My fear of heights has gradually worsened over time and the anxiety I feel has become so numbing that I'd nearly avoid going up a step ladder. But in August 2017, my editor at the time was asked if anyone in the newsroom would be interested in taking part in an abseil, to raise much needed money for charity. The catch was the whole thing would be videoed and published on the *Independent.ie* website.

A colleague and close friend thought it would be funny to put my name forward when nobody else offered. The simple thought of it there and then made my stomach turn, but how could I turn down an opportunity to help young children with life-threatening conditions?

I had a week to mentally prepare – but, truth be told, no amount of time could have helped me. The night before the big event, I also agreed to go for after-work drinks with the same colleague who had put me in this precarious position.

'It will help calm the nerves,' he said.

It did not.

We ended up out until 2.00 a.m. and the fear I felt the next morning had been amplified to the extent that I was considering pulling out. The only thing that stopped me was the fear of feeling my editor's wrath and the guilt of letting down the Make-A-Wish Foundation.

Our office on Talbot Street is about a fifteen-minute walk from the State Street building, which I would soon be dangling from. The nerves combined with the escapades from the night before left me with palpitations that I thought were going to kill me before the abseil did.

When I walked into the lobby of State Street, I ran into an old friend who I happened to meet on a school trip to Lourdes, France when we were seventeen. It was a coincidence that he happened to work there but, me being me, I took it as a sign that I would soon be joining God.

I was told in advance that some famous faces would be taking part including the *X-Factor*'s Mary Byrne. When I arrived, it turned out she could no longer do it that day, and I thought, 'if Mary's not doing it, I'm not doing it'.

We were then brought into a room filled with abseiling equipment. At this point I was flushed in the face and could no longer feel my hands. The next twenty minutes felt like a blur. I could not recall anything that the instructors had said to me and before I knew it, I was standing on the roof of the State Street building wearing a hard hat.

The fresh air to the face was the reality check and I started to have a panic attack. Even looking at the blue cranes across the road made my legs turn to jelly.

'I can't do it, I can't do it,' I told my friend Jason, who I swore would never be my friend again. A young boy who was also participating in the abseil saw how distressed I was and came over to try to comfort me. 'It's going to be fine. If I can do it, so can you,' he said smiling.

Here was a young boy less than half my age who didn't have an ounce of fear in his face. This brave boy, I then learned, was someone who was battling a life-threatening condition and his wish was to abseil down a tall building. Soon everything was put into perspective.

I walked over to the edge of the building to finally do the abseil. I'll never forget looking to my right-hand side and seeing that boy waving at me with a big smile before he jumped with his two feet down the side of the building. Needless to say, my attempt wasn't as seamless and there were a few tears shed, but by refusing to look down at the ground, I somehow managed to find the courage to take that first leap.

The whole thing lasted less than five minutes and the adrenaline I felt almost made me want to get back up there and do it again. Almost.

After finally conquering my fear and feeling immensely proud, I looked around to try to find my colleague Jason who was supposed to be filming the whole thing, but he was nowhere to be seen. I had just thrown myself down the side of a building – something which none of my friends thought I would be brave enough to do – and there was no sign of the person who was meant to capture the proof.

It turns out Jason had somehow managed to get himself trapped on the roof and had missed the whole thing. My first thought was: 'It was all for nothing! I did this for work and now we don't even have a video!' But truth be told, it wasn't about the video for work, this was about doing something out of my comfort zone and helping young children. If it hadn't been for that young boy speaking to me as I battled an anxiety attack, I don't think I would have gone through with it.

He was the truly courageous one.

The video of me freaking out on top of the roof still made it to the *Independent.ie* website, but sadly to this day most people still don't believe that I actually went through with it.

But I know the truth, and I'm really glad that I did.

THE LETTER

Dr Richard Terres

I have an uncomfortable relationship with the post. I can go days, even weeks, without checking my mailbox. I often don't open letters. Bills can marinate for months before being checked. The root cause is pretty simple to understand. It started when my father disappeared.

He didn't actually disappear; he was lost at sea, along with the entire crew. There were seven men aboard, all working on classified Defence Department research, developing underwater communications capabilities for the US government.

The *Marie* set sail on the morning of Tuesday, 7 June 1960, from Santa Barbara Harbour, and was due to return by dusk. When it was late into the night and there was no return, my mom raised an alarm. There ensued a mobilisation of local fishermen, Coast Guard resources and surveillance aircraft. In the week that followed, a few pieces of debris and four bodies were found. My dad was not one of them.

You can probably imagine the media frenzy and attention. I have a difficult time thinking of what my mother was going through. She was 32-years old and had four young children: my older brother was just seven, I was four, my sister, two and my youngest brother, one. Her husband was most likely gone, and any hope was fading with each day that passed. How could she even conceive of what the future had in store? She had no income, and no job; she had been a stay-at-home mom with no college degree and no vocation. I have one daughter, now grown, and it required the constant attention of both my wife and I to take care of her. I can't fathom the effort required having to raise four children under the age of eight.

Local newspapers have since referred to this as one the top stories of the 1960s. It wasn't just the boat disappearance, it was all the speculation around it. The Cold War between the US and Soviet Union was at its height and the Santa Barbara Channel was known to be regularly visited by enemy submarines. Suppositions of hijack and kidnap by hostile agents were a common theory for what happened. There was other speculation that it was the result of a collision with a larger craft, but there were no reports of any incidents. Most of the men on board, including my father, were ex-military, tough and trained divers. If anyone had a chance of surviving and being on one of the several offshore islands, these would have been they guys to do just that.

I don't know what went on in Mom's mind, but she knew she had to get away from all the attention and all the speculation. So, she bundled up the family and headed to the mountains. In the 1930s, her father had built a rustic cabin in the Sierra Nevadas, near Yosemite. It was over a ten-hour drive from our home. The cabin offered no luxuries. Everyone slept outside on the deck. The toilet was in an outhouse. There was no bath or shower. The cooking stove needed to have wood chopped daily to keep it burning. There was running water and electricity, but those were the only amenities.

Mom wanted respite from the constant reminders and questions. At the cabin, she had a known situation that was tough, but she could control. She knew that her family needed insulation from all the speculation and observation. She also knew that she could keep us children engaged and active. There is a nearby lake where we would swim and play in the water daily, and we passed the summer unaware of the turmoil and speculation back home.

We were aware that our dad wasn't with us. I can't say what was in the minds of my siblings; all I can remember is asking my mom, 'Where's Dad?' Her response: 'I don't know, we're waiting for a letter from the Coast Guard.'

The years passed. Dad never showed up. Mom got on with things. She went back to college to get a degree. Life for us kids seemed normal; where normal becomes what you know and do every day. We were absolutely loved and taken care of.

Somehow, she got by.

Somehow, we got by.

We never lacked for affection.

We never lacked for attention.

Mom was a tough taskmaster. We always had chores. We always had obligations. She insisted that we do something cultural, so my sister and younger brother took up Spanish dance (our family's heritage), and I took up piano lessons.

Mom eventually remarried. My stepfather was a wonderful and caring man, but he was eighteen years her senior and had already had his own family. He pretty much left Mom to raise us kids, which she did. Her fervent belief was that boys needed to do outdoor activities – so she taught us how to fish, and she took us backpacking. She was always there to make sure that we were able to do the things we wanted to do.

She taught us snow-skiing at an early age. The logistics involved with getting four young kids kitted out and on the ski-hill would baffle the toughest drill sergeant out there, but not Mom. I clearly remember my first day; I was so frustrated that I vowed to never do it again. Of course, I did stick with it, because of Mom's enthusiasm and persistence. And now that I've slalomed competitively, that first day seems a far, and silly, distant memory.

My mother was the strongest and best person I will ever know. My father and his shipmates have been lauded as heroes that died in the service of their country. But the real heroes were the wives who were

---

left behind and had to pick up the pieces. My mom was the hero. As far as I'm aware, she only cried once – about six weeks after the disappearance, at the check-out till when she was buying groceries. She was overwhelmed by the thought of how much our dad loved his meals. I never heard that story until many years later. Mom never let on that she was hurting. She never showed she was feeling a loss.

Mom's strength was evidenced in her sincerity, her faith and her positivity. I never once heard her moan about things being too much. I never once felt that we lacked for anything. Her super-power was being non-judgemental. She certainly didn't agree with many of my life choices but, nevertheless, always supported me.

I think our family was a success. All four of her kids went to college and have had productive careers. We've all married and had our own kids. Some of the marriages haven't been fully successful, but all of our children are fantastic. I'd like to think that's because we had a pretty good role model for how to raise them.

All in all, I think back on my childhood very warmly. And I don't think I will ever meet anyone the equal of my mother.

But then there is the matter of the post. That letter I was waiting for never came. The Coast Guard never wrote to us. We never knew the fate of our dad. It still haunts me, and each and every one of my siblings. I still can't think or talk about my dad and not tear up. But what remains even stronger is my absolute admiration for my mom. For the strength to know that she had to continue and give us kids hope and courage. I think that's why she deflected and gave me the hope of a letter from the Coast Guard.

And so to this day, I still wait for that letter, but I suspect that if it ever comes, I won't really want to open it.

DAN

Fran Curry

By any measure my childhood was a strange one and, no doubt, I was a strange child. Around the time of my First Holy Communion I went to spend some time with my grandparents, and never went home. My parents were gentle, lovely people who lived in the same town but I suppose one week led to another and then another, until it became the norm.

Even though I was spoilt, I became desperately homesick and missed my mother but, even at that young age, I felt that it would hurt Nanan, as I called her, and my grandfather, if they knew, so I hid my sadness as best I could. At night, however, I cried and, for some reason, became quite obsessed with the notion of death, as I suppose many children do.

My grandfather was quite sick with the doctor coming and going at least once a week, so there was always uncertainty and anxiety. Before you think this is a dark tale, there was consolation.

My solace came from three different sources. Books, mainly the works of Enid Blyton. This was long before she was deemed politically incorrect. There was also music and I discovered at an early age that I had a natural talent which allowed me to play instruments without any tuition. It was a talent I made good use of later in life, going on to be a professional musician and traveling the world for many years.

However, as a child, my greatest saviour was Dan. Without Dan I am not sure how I would have survived.

He wasn't real. Dan was my imaginary friend. He was my sidekick in all sorts of adventures – adventures that generally took place before I fell asleep. Although Dan was strong and capable, there was no doubt that I was the boss and he did my bidding. Whatever adventures I conjured up in my young brain, we were always the heroes. There was never an issue getting me to go to bed because it was then that we took flight to save the country, or even the world if necessary.

As the years went by I lost touch with Dan but even now, in my fifties, I still think of him from time to time. He felt so real. Maybe he was an angel of some kind. I don't know, but I do know that I certainly owe him a great deal for getting me through some tough times.

Angels don't always have wings and – who knows – wherever Dan is, he may well be helping another child through a difficult time right now.

EXPECTING WHAT'S NOT EXPECTED

John Fulham

Expectations were not high.

'Hard Luck, Gerry,' my father was told when he golfed with his friends after I was born.

'We don't know how long Johnny is for this world, so we won't operate,' my mother was told as she waited for me to have surgery that would help me along in the future.

Such were the levels of expectation that people had for me back in 1971 that it is any wonder I achieved anything at all.

Or is it?

I look at my five-year-old son now and marvel at his belief that I and he can do anything. Even when climbing or playing football, he says, 'Come on Dad keep on trying'. He cuts me no slack, and nor should he. For him, my wheelchair is just a way of doing, or achieving, things. His expectations of everything in life know no boundaries, so why should I, or anyone else, accept those boundaries either?

People sometimes ask me what was it like to grow up as a child with a disability? I don't know.

I was just a child growing up, no labels, no restrictions. I climbed trees, went down slides, went to school alongside my friends and adventured wherever they adventured. I had a family who entertained my fantasy that I too could be a Jedi Knight like Luke Skywalker. They encouraged my childhood allowing me to understand that I was unique, and the world was my oyster, and even though I might do things a bit differently, the world was still my oyster, full of my own anticipation and expectation. They allowed me to make a wish to be whatever I wanted to be.

The world around me thought differently, and as I moved into my teens my childhood innocence took a few knocks. I grew older and picked up on the perceptions of the world around me. There were times when I questioned whether I could get a job, whether I could get to live in a place of my own, whether I would ever be able to meet someone and have a family. Would anyone marry somebody with a disability like me? Back then, I did not see many people like me out and about, living their life. Despite my family's belief in me, I lacked the confidence to believe in myself.

But around that time, I discovered sport and along with it those people, the role models who showed me that there was a way to achieve everything I wanted to, even if I could not yet see how. From there, I discovered a world in which everything was possible, that there is always a way and I just needed to reclaim my wish and figure out my own *how*.

When I left home and moved to Dublin, I lived in a two-storey house with a chair upstairs and a chair downstairs. Though the world did not expect me to live away from home, there was a way and I just had to find it. When I went for my interview in the bank, there was just one medical question – 'How will you be able to manage the toilet?' I answered, 'I'll flush it like you do'. People did not expect me to apply for a job, but I did. I developed the confidence not to accept that someone else's expectation for me has to be to be my own.

From there I went on to become a European Champion, European record holder, four-time Paralympian, three-time winner of Dublin Marathon. I became a bank manager, fell in love with a marathon runner, got married, owned my own house and had my own family. My finest achievement is my son, Harry.

There is a joke in my family that men are just little boys in long trousers. I believe that needs to be true for all of us. Though we may grow up and we may grow old, we should never lose sight of our childhood innocence, that belief that you can achieve anything. Though the world around us may still place a limit on what they believe is possible for people with disabilities, I do not! I am making a wish today that my story will inspire you, and anyone who has a doubt. What you expect of yourself will be what counts, and when you have a challenge, there is always a way, it is just a matter of figuring out your own *how*.

My wish is this: may you always keep pushing on those expectations.

WORDS

Áine Toner

Words are my currency. I spend all day, every day with them. Is this the most appropriate wording for a headline? Would a different verb work better there? How many adjectives will I let our feature writers away with? (I'm not a fan of an adjective.)

But while it takes a skill to bring readers into the world of whatever you're writing, I feel there's a particular talent in song writing. Many songs have hardly any words, or the same words, over and over. They run the gamut of emotions within mere minutes: you can go from happy to sad, frustrated to empowered, pessimistic to optimistic when the *right* tune begins to play.

Music has always had the power to make listeners engage, to interact, to feel something. It reminds me of the people I love most – and for that, I'm very grateful.

A small Sydney hotel, 2007. While my friends are out celebrating our youth, I am in bed feeling ill and more than a bit sorry for myself. When they return, they bring grocery shop microwaved nachos – at 2.00 a.m.

– to aid my recovery. Giddy, one of my best friends begins to sing to cheer me up (the nachos not having done the trick). Scissors Sisters' 'I Don't Feel Like Dancing', if you've read this far. It was, and still is, one of my favourite songs.

Said friend swayed and swayed and then there was a small incident with the miniature fridge but she was perfectly fine and now I can never think of that song without remembering that evening. Speaking of Scissors Sisters, another track, 'Only the Horses', reminds me of another best friend and a piece of their writing. When I hear it, no matter the circumstances, I feel closer to her and that I'm not alone.

For me, music is the medium where you can say, 'It's not just me, I'm not the only person feeling this way.' That is powerful and something I cherish.

So many songs in my iTunes library are chosen specifically for whom they remind me of: that Mel C track I skip past for the friend who is no longer in my life but whose favourite song I can't delete; the festive jingle that brings me back to an office environment where another BFF would physically step into the Christmas season; the *Dawson's Creek* tune that keeps a little bit of my favourite show when I was seventeen in my heart indefinitely.

That's not to mention the back catalogues of many an eighties performer (I'm a child of the eighties, I can't help it) and the boyband releases I queued overnight to buy.

Music returns you to an exact moment. I will always be twelve and singing in my friend's bedroom, hairbrush microphone in hand when I hear Let Loose's 'Crazy for You'.

It's not overestimating to say the right music at the right time can make you feel invincible. How many of us have jumped up to a Destiny's Child track, proclaiming that we're independent women? How many have slid to the floor at a wedding to rock the boat with our fellow guests (and often, the bridal party)? How many of us feel like we're starring in our own music video when listening to music on a train or bus and having all the feelings as we stare out the window?

Surely not just me.

In an ocean of podcasts, I will always opt for music when I need a wordy hit when travelling.

My father has always said not to hear music would cause him great unhappiness so it's natural too that I have a particular song that reminds me of my parents, my two favourite people.

'When You Were Sweet Sixteen' is perhaps an unusual choice for someone who wasn't around when this was written or released – but it is my song for Mummy and Daddy Toner, who met in their teens. I cannot listen to it without crying, which isn't ideal on public transport.

Being swept up in a moment, allowing yourself to be carried away by the words or the melody or a singer's intonation, I am all for it.

It is what I turn to when I cannot make sense of what's going on around me. But also when I am happy, or sad, or scared. Angry? I've a track for that. Feeling not quite yourself? Come and listen to my specific playlist.

We cannot change many things in the world but I believe that, as much as possible, we can change how we feel about them. Music helps me to do that.

Bizarrely, my favourite song is one that I rarely listen to, almost the equivalent of your best Sunday dress. Don McLean's 'Vincent' feels so visceral to me that when I occasionally allow it to play without skipping, it's like I'm in a Tardis of memories.

My father carting an A0 print of Van Gogh's painting home, a gift for my eighteenth birthday, on a Belfast bus. Every memory of that signature celebration. I remember listening to Don do his thing as I sat on the lovely looking but highly uncomfortable chairs in our old office as a child, knowing even then that these words held something special for me.

Music won't change events. It can't fix things forever. But momentarily, it will right you. It'll make you feel less alone – and that can be transformative.

So, when you see me, head bopping along to a beat, know that I'm back at an important place or time, and happily reliving it.

OVERCOMING

Dr Sinéad McCoole

In the early years of the twentieth century, Frances Brennan, known then as 'Fanny', grew up in the South Dublin Union workhouse (now St James' Hospital) where over 3,600 men, women and children lived. In the workhouse families were separated; men, women and children living in different buildings of the large Union complex. The poorest of the city, who had come seeking relief from destitution.

Fanny was not separated from her family. Her widowed mother Elizabeth was a ward mistress at the South Dublin Union. We know from census records that Fanny, her sister Lily, her mother, and her maternal grandmother Eliza Butler lived in the Union's officer quarters. Elizabeth's job provided for them all and gave them a place to live, together. While no diaries, memoir or letters of Fanny's early life survive, her formative years must have had an impact as for the rest of her life she worked for the welfare of others. Fanny and her sisters were activists for social change and social justice through writing, lecturing, teaching and advocating. In modern parlance they would be called *change makers*, looking to change the social structure and help vulnerable women and children overcome their difficult circumstances.

Through many, mostly individual acts, such as speaking to select groups, writing articles for journals (albeit with a tiny readership), teaching groups of children, these women made advances, introduced new ideas and changed old ways for the better. They were also part of a changing Ireland, their work intertwined with events shaping modern Ireland.

Fanny adopted the Irish name Áine when she joined the Gaelic League and took lessons in the Irish language. It was through the Gaelic League she met the man Edward Kent, whom she fell in love with and married. Edward is better known as Éamonn Ceannt, a member of the military council that initiated the Irish rebellion of Easter 1916. The provisional government of the Irish Republic issued a proclamation, setting out their beliefs for the Republic, which was addressed to 'Irishmen and Irishwomen' (before women had the right to vote and stand in parliamentary elections). The Proclamation offered equal rights and equal opportunities, pledging to 'cherish all the children of Ireland equally'.

When Éamonn Ceannt was executed by firing squad following the 1916 Rising, Áine was left a young widow; their son a child of ten years. Overcoming her own heartache and sorrow she became a caregiver to many Irish children whose lives were impacted by the years of war that followed the 1916 Rising.

Fanny met her future husband when she had just left school and described their meeting as a 'date of fate'. Her older sister Lily had got seats in a special train carriage carrying Gaelic League teachers from Dublin to Galway. Fanny recalled the sparkling eyes of the teacher from Central Branch, who was able to whistle as 'sweet as a bird'. She watched him get off at stations to speak Irish to those on the platforms. She recollected that the young people, like herself, involved in the Gaelic League were not interested in politics but the language, music, dancing and games. The man she would marry was a shy clerk in the Dublin Rates Office. A gifted piper, he could also play the violin, flute and tin whistle. His love of the Irish language, music and culture would lead him to radical nationalism and revolution. He would die for Ireland.

Fanny's life could have been so different.

Éamonn's courtship letters to Áine survive, housed in the National Library of Ireland. They speak of her tender heart and tellingly, 'the depth of her goodness'. In the fashion of the time her fiancé described himself as her protector, but in time she would become the protector and not the protected.

As the widow of a 1916 Leader, Áine, Bean Éamonn Ceannt travelled all over Ireland, year after year distributing money which had been raised to help children affected by 'wars in Ireland'. Some were orphaned, most were children with widowed mothers, whose fathers had died in violent circumstances. Sometimes the children had witnessed violence and the burning of their homes, others were the victims of violence. The year 1920 was described as 'The Year of Terror'.

The original fundraising had been carried out in the United States of America. By 1921 it was reported that five million dollars had been raised. Firstly, it was distributed through the White Cross, but when this was wound up in the 1920s the White Cross Committee for the Maintenance of Children then became the Children's Relief Committee and continued the work for 1,000 children. James Webb was Chairman, Nannie O'Rahilly Treasurer, Kathleen Clarke Secretary and Áine Ceannt the Administrator. For twenty-seven years, at their offices in Room 7 of 27 Dawson Street, Dublin, Áine and her colleagues led the work to guide these children to adulthood. It was said that Áine was the face of organisation '… administering, mothering, guiding and admonishing year after year with wisdom, knowledge and sympathy'.

She recalled visiting large families in the country with children and animals running about as she arrived. Her visits must have caused excitement and fear, alongwith anticipation following her letter to the family that she was coming from Dublin. She was there to evaluate claims, to check if the child in question was eligible for aid. As she was given space to sit down and speak to the child, one can imagine the anxious wait of a mother in an adjoining room, the children supressing the natural inclination to be boisterous, the barking of animals and the sounds of the farm. She would have needed to focus closely on the child, to listen attentively to their words, to determine if this child required her help. It could have been assistance for medical needs, or for further education. Besides a basic allowance there were so many demands. So often the choices were difficult, with limited funds, how to choose those most in need? She knew, and everyone who applied knew, that her actions were simply life-changing. It was for so many a time of real want, in the Ireland of the 1920s, 1930s and 1940s.

Receipt of ongoing support for education depended on good results and we know the children's grades were inspected. Number 7 was a small office, and you can imagine the apprehension of mothers or guardians, and more so the children, when they were summoned to explain a misdemeanour or poor school results. Children were also assisted with medical needs, securing houses, apprenticeships, and jobs. We know some became government officials, clerks and teachers while others entered religious life.

When Áine Ceannt wrote *The Story of the Irish White Cross 1920–1947** there are only tiny glimpses of her own story – her thoughts and feelings were not articulated. I am sure even with friends she did not discuss the children the committee supported; knowing the cost it had taken for people to confide in her their needs, their difficult circumstances.

In 1947 when the offices closed, she took down the pictures that adorned the walls; the pictures of boys in suits, girls in their First Holy Communion finery, and portrait photographs of proud young men and women who attained their first job or completed their education. Some of the pictures were reproduced in *The Story of the Irish White Cross 1920–1947*. The pictures of the children are described for example as 'a trio from the Kingdom of Kerry' and 'a girl from the County of Clare'. I have never found an account written by any of the children. They did not speak publicly (and often their descendants are unaware) about the funding from the Children's Relief Committee.

Áine was known as 'Little Áine' by her husband because of her petite stature, which made her sound fragile. She was in fact the opposite – strong and determined, and she fought for the children in her care.

During the early years of self-government in Ireland there were women like Áine Ceannt who did what they could for the welfare of others, doing what was possible with what little they had. They witnessed the effects of poverty, war and suffering and worked to overcome difficulties, to solve problems where they could and help to make a better future for those in their care.

Published by the Candle Press, Fleet Street, Dublin at the Sign of the Three Candles (1947)

MOLLY

Carol Dooley

My godmother, Molly, always thought there was nothing that a cup of tea and a banana sandwich couldn't resolve. Well, to be fair, I'm not sure if that's exactly what she thought. However, every afternoon after school I would go to her house where she would serve up tea in dainty bone china cups and always with banana sandwiches – mashed not sliced, and with a touch of sugar for added sweetness!

As we sipped and munched I would regale her with the ups and downs of my day and she would, in turn, put my little world to rights. Molly wasn't a blood relative and how she came to be my godmother I never did find out. She was nonetheless very much family, close friends with my gran and part of a circle of truly great women of a certain age who saw to it that I was kept safe and secure. Women from a different era who asked for little and expected less, but who were always joyous, fun and fiercely loyal to those they loved.

I had siblings and there were lots of cousins, but to Molly I knew I was extra special. Maybe I was the child she never had. I was of course too young to realise it, but she was my champion, my confidante and my *bestest* friend. She was also the one who instilled in me a lasting love of radio.

Every afternoon without fail we would listen to the day's instalment of BBC Radio 2's soap opera *Waggoner's Walk*. I didn't always understand what was going on but I remember loving the intimacy of it. For those fifteen minutes everything would be put on hold as Molly and I lost ourselves in the world of the residents of the fictional cul de sac. Then after tea, it was time for David Hamilton!

I was captivated by the magic of it all. Why her radio loyalty never extended to RTÉ I have no idea but I resolved from that time that come hell or high water I was going to work for the BBC one day. Molly told me that was a great plan and I like to think she had a big part in that when it eventually happened a few years after she passed away.

Sometimes I'd run to her after some silly row at home and again, over a cup of tea and a banana sandwich, it would all get sorted. She knew everything there was to know about me because there was nothing I didn't tell her. My tragedy, however, is that I knew so little about her, and those who could have enlightened me have all now sadly passed too.

She never married and while there was a rumour of a fiancé killed in the war, I never asked, probably because I was afraid it might be true. Molly died when I was just twelve years old and I clearly remember sitting in the back of the church dry eyed and emotionless, in retrospect failing to grasp the enormity of her loss.

Years later, while living in America, I became friends with Liz, a woman who claimed to be psychic. One day she told me she'd had a visit from a kindly elderly woman from my past who had a message for me. She wanted me to know she was always beside me and was always looking out for me. A fairly generic message so I took it with a pinch of salt. But a couple of days later Liz told me she'd had another visit from the same elderly woman with an additional message, one that Liz said she couldn't quite understand but that she promised to pass on. It was to remind me to never forget the banana sandwiches ...

CAROL DOOLEY

One Man and His Dog

Archbishop Michael Jackson

A man and his family once had a small dog. The dog was devoted to all members of the family equally. The dog was easy-going, willing to take a walk, willing to sit and watch the humans watch television, willing to go on adventures that were shared with the humans. He trusted them and they loved him. But it was not possible for the dog and the humans to hold a conversation about what they had all been doing or watching or seeing. The one thing they had in common was that they all ate but the dog was puzzled that he liked their food, and they did not like his food, however hard he tried to share.

Dogs and humans speak differently. Dogs and humans communicate differently. They each communicate with their own species, but they have not yet worked out how to speak to one another. At the same time, it is possible for them to understand one another with a shared and unforced instinct of belonging to each other. This was not a massive problem for any of them because their relationship was not about talking and arguing, but about listening and understanding.

Compiled by Brendan Power

One day the man could not get out of bed because he was sick, not in a serious way but he just could not lift his head from the pillow because he ached all over, and the bed was the only place to be. It was warm and it was safe. The other members of the family had gone off to school and off to work so the man was all alone. As he went back to sleep for the third or the fourth time, he heard claws scratching their way up the wooden stairs and he wondered what was happening. It was a sound that he had not heard before but, because he was at home and felt safe, he simply waited to see what happened next. The door of the bedroom pushed open and in came the dog and waited patiently by the side of the bed where the man was lying.

Not only did the man lift the dog up gently and carefully, but the dog knew exactly where he was going next. He climbed from the duvet on to the pillows and wrapped himself round the neck of the man like a blanket. While the man knew that he ached all over, he realized from the healing touch of the dog that it was his neck that ached the most. The warmth of the dog spoke of more than heat. It spoke of devotion and care and of practical response. The man could have asked himself, or even asked the dog: why are you here? How did you know I was sick? And: how did you know that I was in this room? But, why would he do this? There was no need. There was no point. He knew – and he was sure the dog knew – that while they could communicate, they could not question one another in this sort of way. But then he went on to say to himself silently: but does it really matter? This little dog understands me more than I can ever understand him or perhaps myself. Why would I question him? I would not even be able to understand the answer were he able to speak. Here I am. Let me simply enjoy being here and having the dog wrapped around my neck and let me let him help me to get better.

Things improved for the man, and he quickly recovered. The dog stuck with him and with the other members of the family. He continued to do what they did. Sometimes they noticed and sometimes they didn't. But the man did not forget the instinct for kindness shown him by the dog. They did not need to talk but they could certainly communicate with each other. Whether anyone else noticed or not – sure it really did not matter.

DAVID

Lynda Bryans and Mike Nesbitt

Everybody knows children can die of cancer. Don't they? Actually, it's not quite everyone. Billy McCrory was in his forties before he found out, and the voyage of discovery was quite a shock. He was visiting a colleague in hospital when he spotted a young man in another ward, with a Liverpool FC scarf draped over the end of his bed. So, next day Billy tied his Manchester United scarf around his neck before he set off and waved it in mock aggression through the ward window at the young man. He did it again the next day and the next, but on the day after that, he arrived to find the bed was empty. He asked the nurse what had happened. Had the boy been discharged or moved to another ward? The answer was flabbergasting: he had had leukaemia and had passed away overnight.

In that moment, or rather the moment Billy recovered sufficiently from the shock, he transformed from one of many, many decent middle-aged men from east Belfast into a hero, not just to us but to dozens of families struggling to accept the inexplicable misfortune of having a child diagnosed with cancer. Billy set up Shine a Light, a charity dedicated to providing special trips and treats to young people with cancer, and their families. He took young people and their parents to the great football stadia in England and Scotland; to London's finest theatres; he had them picked up in stretch limos and taken to lunch in Belfast's best restaurants. He even organised respite breaks in Salou, Spain and an annual Christmas trip to Lapland. He was a bright beacon in an otherwise dull and potentially depressing landscape.

We first spoke to Billy by telephone. His call was immaculately timed, coming the morning after we had had a detailed chat about our work-life balance, concluding we wanted more balance, less work. UTV was far from a nine to five, Monday to Friday gig. Every fortnight, we flew to England for a few days to record *Sunday Morning*, the ITV network religious affairs programme; we had two young boys of primary school age who never knew who was going to pick them up, where they were going, or when they would get home. On top of that, we had our charity work; anyone who has a public profile will get the opportunity to do good, not least by helping charities, and between us we had a quite a collection of Patron and President titles, picked up in a totally random, piecemeal manner, with the result being there was barely a weekend when at least one of us was not out supporting the third sector.

It was not fair to PJ and Chris, so that night, we decided we should be more strategic, focusing on three charities, one each individually, and one together, offering them all a set number of days on a *use them or lose them* basis. What a splendidly logical conclusion to our chat! It didn't last eighteen hours. It should have, because we should have politely declined Billy's invitation to us to join his fundraising pub quiz, but there was something compelling about Billy McCrory. Even as we said 'Yes', our brains were screaming 'Noooo!'

A pub quiz? We don't do pub quizzes! We did it anyway. The silver lining was that the pub was in Ballyhackamore, just around the corner from where we lived. *The Point* helped lead the way in developing the area into such a mecca for eating and drinking that it's now nicknamed *Bally-snack-amore*. It was a two-story bar/restaurant with a pointy, spire-like lid and a fashionably wood and steel interior – although a £1 plastic bucket was to be a key feature of the night. The pub was crowded when we arrived, and Billy was all over us within a millisecond. The moustache and lived-in face gave him a stern appearance, he had a frame that suggested he was not to be messed with, but the enduring and enchanting characteristic was his focus on the children. He greeted us, directed us to the last empty table in the bar, and asked who else we had invited to be on Team UTV. This, of course, was the first time Billy had mentioned that we should bring a team. We were trailing after round one, failed to improve our position in round two, struggled in round three, and finished last. To add insult to injury, Billy then took the microphone to thank everyone, picked up his £1 bucket saying he was coming around for contributions, and announced he was leaving the final word to ... us!

We were both quiet on the drive home, probably traumatised. We started talking about last weekend, when a charity had sent a driver to pick us up, transport us to a swanky hotel half an hour away, where we were wined and dined at the top table in return for us doing nothing more productive than drawing the ballot and saying a few words that had been scripted for us by the charity's communications team, before being driven home again.

The more we thought about it, and the contrast with what had just happened, the more we liked Billy McCrory; if it was a question of our dignity versus a pound for a child with cancer, there was only going to be one winner.

If you asked us what was the best thing we ever did during thirteen years at UTV, we are surprised to conclude it has nothing to do with broadcasting. It was something that started with another Billy McCrory phone call. We were making our way from the newsroom to make-up when Maggie at the reception desk waved her phone at us: 'It's a guy called Billy McCrory'. Mike took it, just to tell him we didn't have time to talk and would call back later, but he launched into the story of David Gillespie and he couldn't be stopped. David was a teenager from Strabane, was suffering from leukaemia and was a massive fan of Mickey Harte and his Tyrone Gaelic Football Team, the one that had just fought their way into the 2003 All-Ireland senior football final. Mike needed to end the conversation and get ready for the news. This was our out, because we both knew for a fact there were no tickets available for the match.

That was not the point. As Billy pointed out, forcefully, David did not need a ticket, because he already had one. The issue was that David was too ill to travel to Dublin for the match, so Billy's request wasn't for a ticket, it was to get David to a training session ahead of the game.

We spoke to Adrian Logan in the UTV Sports Department. Logie was our 'Mr GAA'. He phoned the Tyrone Manager, Mickey Harte, suggesting he give him permission to bring David and his parents to the media day. Mickey said no, only because it would be a scrum and no fit place for a very ill young man in a wheelchair. Mickey told Logie instead to invite the Gillespies to a private training session in Omagh the following week. It turned out the Gillespies were the only people in Healy Park that night who were not part of the official structure. David sat and drank in everything. It was the very definition of what Billy was about, providing a special memory money could not buy. When the squad finished, Mr and Mrs Gillespie took David back to the car park for the half-hour drive home, but they were intercepted by a county official who wondered what they doing? They explained they were there by invitation. The official said he knew that, what he meant was what were they doing in the car park. 'Going home,' was the answer. 'No, you're not,' was the response.

The Gillespies were taken into a lounge to await the team, who were getting changed. When they joined the family, they gave David a match ball, signed a team shirt, and one player, Eoin Mulligan, told David that if he scored at Croke Park, David would see him celebrate by punching the air and if David saw that, he would know the goal was for him. David left Healy Park feeling like a prince.

On 28 September 2003, the 116th All-Ireland Senior Football Final finished Armagh 0–9 Tyrone 0–12. Tyrone won the Sam Maguire Cup for the first time in the county's history. David watched the match on television in the family home off the Melmount Road, then went upstairs to bed, as it turned out for the last time. He passed away soon afterwards.

Mickey Harte had placed one condition on David's invitation to Healy Park; he didn't want to read about David's passing in the local newspaper. He wanted a call. When David died, Billy McCrory was one of the first to know. He phoned us, we called Adrian Logan and Logie contacted Mickey Harte, who was on a coach with his victorious team somewhere in County Tyrone. I don't know where they headed, but they never got there. When Mickey Harte took the call, he made his way to the coach driver and told him to turn around and head for Strabane.

The Gillespies were holding a wake for David, whose open coffin was upstairs while downstairs was crowded with grieving relatives and friends. There was a knock at the door and David's mother opened it. There, standing on her doorstep in his match day suit was Mickey Harte. He stood back to reveal the entire Tyrone All-Ireland winning team, also in their match day suits, asking permission to come in and pay their respects. They had left the Sam Maguire in the coach, but on request they brought the trophy in and held it over David's coffin.

We asked Mickey Harte about it all when we made a documentary about Billy a couple of years later. He told us he wanted the team to have some perspective on what they had achieved.

Sport is a nonsense, an important nonsense, but nonsense nevertheless ...

Béal Na Bláth:
A Place of Death and Division
Woodfield:
A Place of Birth and Joy

Helen Collins

My granduncle, Michael Collins, was born on the family homestead of Woodfield, near Clonakilty, on Thursday, 16 October 1890.

He died at Béal na Bláth on 22 August 1922, just short of his thirty-second birthday. In August 2022 the country commemorated the one hundredth anniversary of his death.

Michael was the eighth, and youngest, child of Michael Collins senior and Mary Ann O'Brien. My grandfather, Johnny Collins, was young Michael's older brother by twelve years. Their father, Michael senior, died when young Michael was just seven years old, and their mother, Mary Ann, died ten years later, when Michael was seventeen.

As was the tradition, my grandfather Johnny (known to us as 'Grandy'), as the oldest son, became the owner of Woodfield. Margery Forester in her biography of Michael Collins describes what Woodfield meant to him; 'The way of life at Woodfield in which Michael Collins was to spend his childhood is a key to all that he was later to become. No other single influence was to be closer to his heart. The Woodfield acres were too few to have contained a vision as broad as he possessed, yet to the end of his life they filled it completely'.

Grandy married Katti Hurley, and together they had nine children, eight of whom lived. The youngest child, Liam, my father, was born in 1920 and was the last Collins to be born in Woodfield. Tragedy struck Woodfield in 1921. First, my grandmother, Katti, died of TB, at the young age of thirty-eight. My father was just over twelve months old at the time of her death.

Two short months later, on 7 April 1921, a detachment of soldiers from the Essex Regiment, under the command of Captain A E Percival, arrived at Woodfield and, at bayonet point, forced a number of neighbours to pile hay inside the house, douse it with petrol, and set the house and outbuildings on fire. Even my father's baby cradle was thrown into the flames.

On the same day, Grandy was returning from a meeting in Cork and was taken off the train at Shannonvale, arrested and imprisoned on Spike Island. The children, including my Dad the baby, were left parentless and scattered to the four winds to live with neighbours and relatives.

These huge events have left a traumatic mark on my family to this day.

Michael was devastated to learn of the burning of Woodfield and said, 'they knew where they could hurt me most'. He spent what was to be his last Christmas (1921) at Woodfield, and he and Grandy climbed a nearby hill together on Christmas morning. Michael returned to Woodfield on Thursday 15 June 1922, where he was photographed on the front step of the burnt-out house. His last visit was on that fateful day, Tuesday 22 August 1922, when he made a quick stop to see Grandy and other friends and relatives on his way back to Cork through Béal na Bláth.

Since his death on that day, he has been the person much spoken of, deeply missed and forever absent from our family. It felt to me, growing up, as if his place was set at the table and he just never came home! The feeling was of sadness and loss.

I was much older before I developed a realisation that I had been raised in a home of forgiveness and understanding. I suppose I had taken it for granted and did not realise, until I was older, that such big traumas and loss can also lead to hatred and division. My father, Liam, never promoted or supported such negative thoughts or feelings. He in fact proactively encouraged tolerance, understanding and forgiveness. He never sought to blame or seek out those involved in the ambush at Béal na Bláth. He took the view that a tragic Civil War was taking place and that it was an inevitable heart-breaking consequence of war that people died. He strongly believed that this would have been his uncle Michael's view. This he learned from his father. In fact, a number of the Béal na Bláth ambush party had gone to Grandy and sought, and were given, forgiveness by him.

Throughout his life, my father Liam did everything possible to heal divides, culminating in his Reconciliation Celebration in Woodfield for the centenary of Michael Collins birth in 1990, where, in the presence of the President of Ireland and many distinguished guests, he named his special guests as Síle de Valera and Sir Nicholas Finn, the British ambassador.

When asked by the Béal na Bláth Committee to speak at the annual memorial service on behalf of the Collins family, I accepted the honour mainly on behalf of my father.

Over the years, many wonderful people have spoken at Béal na Bláth, including powerful contributions made by Lord David Putnam, former president Mary Robinson, the late Brian Lenihan and President Michael D Higgins. I think my father, his uncle Michael and my grandfather would have been proud.

My father described his uncle Michael as the man 'whose name has, with the passage of time, come to be respected as an honoured Irish States Man, of and for all the people'.

My father proudly handed over Woodfield to the State in 1991. Thirty years later, my siblings and I were equally proud, in November 2021, in Woodfield, to hand over our granduncle Michael's work diaries to Taoiseach Micheál Martin, who received them on behalf of the Irish people.

In a heartfelt effort to bring reconciliation to painful past events and on behalf of the Collins', I was particularly delighted and honoured to invite Taoiseach Micheál Martin and Tanaiste Leo Varadkar to speak at Béal na Bláth in the centenary year, as a steppingstone towards laying Civil War politics to rest.

FINN

Damien Tiernan

L ife, for all of us, is a series of stories. We all have stories to tell, and
listening the stories of others is one of the greatest privileges any
broadcaster can have.

In my work as a radio broadcaster, I have come across stories of
courage and determination, and we have had the privilege of helping,
and continuing to help, people realise their dreams. This comes from
my innate sense of what journalism should be, being a tribune of the
people – as George Orwell once wrote – and allowing people to tell their
stories through you.

During my time as RTÉ South East Correspondent, where the same
principle applied, I was one of the first to interview Finn, a young Waterford boy who was battling cancer. We did a *Nationwide* piece on him and
the fundraising efforts by the Carrick-on-Suir Motor Club, and others,
to help pay for his treatment and travel, etc. His story grew as he grew,
and his battles proved to be truly inspirational for others. When he rang
the bell in Crumlin, to signify the end of his arduous treatment, a great

many tears were shed by a great many people. Following his recovery, he shared his story with the nation, on *The Late Late Toy Show* where his bravery and his personality, inspired many more.

He then went on to become Grand Marshall for the St Patrick's Day Parade in Waterford!

Fortunately, he is in good health now and his family deserve massive credit for everything they have done to support him and help him through the bad times.

I'm delighted to be associated with Make-A-Wish Ireland for the purposes of this book, where Finn's story and many more from around the country, are based on love, hope and courage – the ingredients of life.

CRISIS OR CHALLENGE?

Neil Bannon

'There is nothing permanent except change' – *Heraclitus*

We regularly hear that we are in a time of crisis. Indeed, it seems we are on a constant run of crises, each one feeling more challenging than the last. Perhaps the reality is that life is all about change, and that embracing the changes life throws at us may lead to a happier and more fulfilling career and existence.

I have been working for over 30 years and running businesses for eighteen of those. During that period, interest rates have been as high as fourteen percent, and less than zero, I have paid taxes as high as 60 percent, and as low as ten percent, worked in an economy that contracted by ten percent in one year and grew by 30 percent in another, hired people when unemployment was sixteen percent, and when it was four percent.

During my career, I have experienced the Irish Punt currency crisis, the launch of the Euro, the Celtic Tiger, Y2K, the Dotcom crash, 9/11, three wars in the Middle East and two in Europe, the Great Global Recession, Covid-19 and the latest crisis: the 2022 cost-of-living crisis. As I hope to be around for a few more years, I confidently expect a few more surprises are in store for me.

When I started in the early 1990s we still used a fax machine and there was a telex machine in the corner, although I wasn't sure what it did. The iPhone wasn't even a twinkle in Steve Jobs' eye. By contrast, for the much of last few years, we have had the entire team seamlessly remote working, attending virtual meetings, and cooperating on projects over the web.

When we set up Bannon in January 2005 we didn't expect to be entering the deepest recession in living memory just three years later, and within five years of setting up Sigma, we didn't expect to be sending everyone to work from home. My father set up his first business in the late seventies and I recall stories he told me of waiting for six months for a telephone line to be installed, of bank strikes that meant no cash flow, of port strikes that meant no fuel, and of 65 percent tax rates.

When you put all of this together, it seems that the only constant really is change, and expecting things to continue as they are for a protracted period is both naïve and, potentially, limiting. If we treat every change and challenge as a crisis, we risk reacting with panic and without fore-thought. We should not only accept that whatever assumptions we have made will be wrong, but relish the opportunity that comes with the knowledge that most other people's assumptions will also be flawed. As technology has speeded up processes, there is a danger in allowing the speed of these processes to control our strategic vision, as opposed to using the nimbleness that the technology facilitates to keep us on course to our strategic goals.

I was recently on a sailing trip with friends and was struck by the constant need to adjust course to reflect the changes in wind, tides and, most importantly, the presence of other boats. The destination remained the same throughout the journey, but the route to get there had to constantly be adjusted to reflect the conditions and realities around us. It is no different in business, or in life. We start by setting our goals. If we don't, we won't know whether we are still en route to achieving them, let alone know when we get there. It is important to recognise that whatever plans we have made to achieve these goals will have to be constantly rewritten as life throws another curve ball at us.

Stop thinking in terms of crisis and panic, and more along the lines of challenges and opportunities. Despite the fact that we live in a world that provides immediate information and answers, it should not distract us from planning for, and thinking of, the long term.

Too often, we tend to focus on problems we can't influence. If we focus on the ones we can have an impact on, we have the makings of a plan.

Once we cease to be scared of the next crisis it is extremely liberating. Problems that once got us down will just become puzzles to solve. These can be large problems such as how to pay the wages this month or deal with a hungry bank, but ultimately there is always a solution and devising a successful solution to what may have seemed an overwhelming problem is one of the most rewarding things any of us will ever do.

Identify the problem, develop the solution, and implement it. If you are in business, make sure that you sell the solution for a price that reflects the value of the problem you are solving. Solving relevant problems can be intellectually, financially, and perhaps even spiritually, rewarding.

The more others talk of crises, and baulk at the prospect of change, the greater the opportunity will be for those who embrace change and see each supposed crisis as just another problem to solve.

THE WOODEN BOX

Mícheál Ó Scannáil

The smell of freshly cut timber is exactly as I remembered. It always reminded me of the saw dust on the floor of Jimmy's butchers in Arklow, where my mam brought me sometimes as a chap. It was the kind of distracting smell that you could listen to with your nose – although finding a distraction was never a problem for me.

Room 309 in Gorey Community School – Charlie Lyon's woodwork class – was more than just the venue for us to work on our Leaving Cert construction projects after school. It was a formulative cradle, where aside from distracting us from the study we weren't doing for our exams, all aspects of life and love in the microcosm of eighteen-year-old boys were discussed and debated. Returning for a visit, I feel like I'm back in my boyish days of wonder here, where every day felt like a new chapter in an engrossing book that would never end. Simultaneously though, it reminds me how, in only a few short years, my universe has expanded past what was happening in front of my nose, to a cosmos of international issues, complex relationships and the reality of death. And the reality of debt. I feel old.

It's difficult for the memories not to come back, standing here. I try to resist the allure of drifting into a rapture of nostalgia – it's my first time back here since *it* happened and I'm still not sure I can handle my emotions – but I can't stop the memories flooding in. I bury the thought of us, only as boys, walking up the town with a box on our shoulders, back into the annals of my subconscious.

Young men should not have to carry boxes on their shoulders.

Sixth Year was hurtling towards its explosive end when last I sat here, and my school years were in their winter. In the summer I would face the biggest challenge of my life to that point – securing the affections of Rachel Duke, before she left for UCD, and found exotic boys, from Cavan or Mullingar.

I was working on hand-turned spindles for my Construction project – a baby's crib – when Darragh Hughes, presumably with hurley in hand, slagged me about Rachel's interest in other boys. While smiling on the outside, all of my pubescent insecurities allowed me to believe him, winding me tighter than the lathe I was using. In my impressionable state of constant uncertainty though, he reassured me that actually she wasn't *that* far out of my league. Seven years later it feels closer-plotted on my timeline that I use that crib, than when the confidence Hughsey instilled in me worked on my now girlfriend, that euphoric summer all those years ago.

The reminiscent smile on my face, though, begins to disappear at the memory of that long walk on the dreariest of days. I can still feel the hard timber digging into my shoulder, as through a huge crowd, we walked the loneliest walk. Surrendering to your emotions is always healthy – I had to learn that the hard way – but this isn't the time or place. I push back.

It's often you hear how profound an impact a teacher has had on a person's life, but Charlie Lyons' classroom feels like the fulcrum of my lived experience, all the big moments of my life tracing back in one way or another.

It was actually Charlie who convinced me to pursue journalism. Even though I was pretty good at woodwork, he recognised an A in his subject as a platform for the points I needed to do something altogether different. So well informed, he showed me the value of news and after being told to lower my ceiling by a guidance counsellor, Charlie told me to blow the roof off instead. He's still the first person to message me when I make achievements in my career.

It might be just the knack of congenial people to make you feel like your presence has an impact on them, but I always felt that Charlie had an affinity with our class in particular. Even now as I stand in the light, airy space, filled with heavy, mallet-weathered tables, the walls are covered with photos. Many are of me and my friends.

One of the photos on the wall is of Paul Boyle, Darragh Bellanova, Chris Martin and me. It was the first time I'd been in this room. While the former duo were already my best friends, myself and Chris had a love–hate relationship. Contenders for the Gorey RFC scrum-half jersey, and in different streams in school, we were always in competition. During those few weeks in Transition Year though, when the four of us shirked class to make props for the school musical, Chris joined the others as one of my best friends. We messed as we constructed a huge MDF cross for the church scene in *Footloose*. My eyes water as I recall the journey from Esmond Street to Gorey Little Theatre as we purposely carried the cross through the crowds on the main street, revelling in the confusion of passersby, laughing all the way with the wooden box on our shoulders.

Young men should not have to carry boxes on their shoulders.

My relationship with Chris continued to bloom and when we were both put into Charlie's class for Leaving Cert Construction, it had blossomed in all its glory. Construction after school every day, and then up to the club for training, we were inseparable.

The memory I have been trying to avoid is becoming inescapable, until I notice a *Construction Studies Today* book opened on the concrete chapter. I am relieved to be reminded of one of the funniest mornings I ever had. Charlie was irritated that morning. He arrived in class more agitated than he would usually be, even when all hell was breaking loose in class. We were learning about concrete, and for concrete to set without big air gaps, it has to be vibrated. Just like Charlie knew exactly what would happen if you leaned too hard on a chisel, or wore loose clothes next to the pillar drill, his years of experience told him what was coming, having to explain *vibrators* to a class full of eighteen-year-old boys, with a scattering of girls of the same age.

Everything he said seemed to be an innuendo, and Charlie had to use his rare but stern yell to disrupt sniggering throughout. Luke and Paul Murphy – not related but sharing the same sense of devilment – tested the boundaries. When Charlie explained that leaving the vibrator in too long makes the concrete too wet, it was game over for that lesson. I never saw Chris laugh as hard as that day, as our beloved teacher scrambled to regain our attention.

It was Chris' sense of fun and joy that made him different to everyone else. It's a very Irish thing to say, *nobody had a bad word to say about him*, but in a culture where bavardage only stops where scandal begins, it is a genuine compliment. It couldn't be truer about Chris.

Charlie is talking about him now, as he always makes a point of doing. He's laughing sentimentally about all of Chris' mishaps. Calamity always followed where Chris went, but he laughed it off, which made it funny for everyone else too. As Charlie continues though, my smile pouts and begins to quiver.

Just like at the time, trying to suppress this feeling only leads to an explosion of emotion. I'm being transported back to that day – the worst day of my life.

I threw away the phone in disbelief when Rachel called with the news that morning. It couldn't be real. When all the lads met up, it still wasn't real. Until Darragh Hughes arrived and burst out with, 'What the feck is going on?' His evident moment of realisation legitimised what was, until then, a truth too hard to believe. I was broken. We all were.

I can't remember what the weather was like, but as we walked down Esmonde Street it may as well have been pouring rain, there was no capacity for sunshine in my heart. I could hear the pulsating of blood in my head, which felt heavy and tight, like someone had clamped my scalp in one of 309's bench vices. Everything stood still as my brain attempted to process how I felt. Sam O'Gorman was always a voice of reason and a trustworthy confidant in the days of Room 309, but as we changed into suits in his house, we couldn't speak a word. I didn't know what to say. I didn't even know how I felt. Not palpably sad, though that came in a torrent later, just empty. Confused.

Outside of St Michael's Church, everyone stared as we, as young men, again carried a wooden box through the crowds. This time though, their attention was the last thing we wanted. I understood why they all looked at us with sympathy and touched our backs when we passed, but I wanted them all to go away. We were all there, only Chris was in the box.

Weeping now in Room 309.

Young men should not have to carry boxes on their shoulders.

Tea With Dad

Kate Durrant

This is about some mugs, and my Dad, and coincidence – or maybe about something that is so much more than mugs, and Dads, and coincidences.

I was blessed to have my Dad spend the last year of his life with me and my young children, it was a beautiful challenge as young and old learned from each other and fought over the remote control in those days of a one television house. They adored their granddad and hung off every word of his outrageous tales, and when I questioned the prudence of sharing those stories with those impressionable young ears he would smile. 'A cautionary tale, my pet, a cautionary tale,' he would reassure me, with a laugh that belied any apology.

He backhanded them with, what seemed to small people, vast sums of money, with all denying it as hands were hidden behind backs and smiles masked with outraged denial, and a beautiful unholy alliance was formed between the people who were the bookends of my life.

He travelled light, arriving with little but the paraphernalia of his advanced illness, an old biscuit tin crammed with sepia photographs of unidentified relatives, and a set of four fine bone china mugs. Not particularly nice mugs but, as Dad reminded me on more than one occasion, expensive mugs that he had purchased one at a time over a series of weeks.

My lovely Dad died in 2006 leaving my heart broken, my children bereft, the photographs in the tin still nameless and the mugs, which I really didn't like, hanging off a wooden tree in the kitchen.

I put them away and over the years when I occasionally took them out intending to get rid of them I could see my wonderful Dad, week after week, taking his time, making his choice before placing the mug carefully into his shopping trolley. Each time they went back into the cupboard. But eventually I Marie Kondo'd them, thanked them for their service and, with no small tug in the chest area, wrapped them carefully and gave them away to the local charity shop.

During the summer, at a site meeting with a client, I opened the canteen cupboard in their warehouse to find Dad's mugs staring back at me. Not mugs like them, but the exact mugs. That same set of four fine bone china mugs that Dad had picked out so carefully, week after week, all those years ago.

No one could explain where they had come from or how they happened to be there so, needless to say, they are now back at home where they belong, and I'm sitting watching the new day dawn and enjoying a mug of tea with my Dad.

My Four-Legged Friends

Orlaith Frawley

In 1990, when I was just twelve years old, I was diagnosed with a tumour on the stem of my brain. It had been misdiagnosed for the previous three years, making the operation to remove it very precarious, and leaving us all very thankful for the skill of neurologist Pat O'Neill in the Mater Hospital. Even after the operation, there were concerns as to whether I would survive – I had lost my gag reflex, my lungs had collapsed, I actually died on two occasions but was brought back by resuscitation, and then spent the next few months on a ventilator.

Even though I did regain full consciousness, I had to remain on the flat of my back for almost a year. With my lungs not working properly, it was necessary to have a tracheostomy, which involved making an incision in my neck and inserting a tube directly into my windpipe to help me breathe. I was constantly attached to drips, tubes, needles – in fact, you name it, I had it! The doctors had not given my folks any hope at all that I was going to have any quality of life, never mind survive, but somehow my stubbornness pulled me through.

With no voice, I had to communicate using a keyboard and, as I slowly started to recover, my folks granted me a wish. I thought about it for a while and then told them what I wanted. I don't remember exactly what they said or did, but to say they were surprised would be an understatement. I could not understand their reaction. After all, they had asked me what I wanted and, as far as I was concerned, it was no big deal to wish for a horse.

The sticking point, however, was that at that point there was no way in the world any doctor was going to let me get anywhere near a horse. Fortunately, Dad saw it differently, saying, 'I'd prefer to see her dead in a ditch, than in a hospital bed'.

It was another year or so before I got out of that bed and learned how to walk again. I was still on oxygen the odd time and had the tracheostomy for another four years after that, but I was sticking to my guns, I really wanted to sit on a horse. Dad took me to stables where I had three instructors holding on to me, and it must have been obvious to everyone just how much I enjoyed it, because I got to go again, and again, and again. My folks really are incredible people, Mam's so predictable and caring, while Dad was more like me, chance it and have the craic! Sadly, he is no longer with us.

Whenever I could, I would go down to the stables, just to brush the horses, and be around them. Over a period of months and years, I gradually got stronger, until eventually I reached the point where I got to ride independently. Wow! The freedom! There was nothing like it. There was something magical about sitting on this incredible animal.

Nine years after my operation, against all the odds, I celebrated my twenty-first birthday, and guess what I got? Yes; my very own horse. There is just something so soothing about these beautiful animals. I had been through every emotion you can think of and had no idea why I was feeling so anxious and confused, but they gave me back my confidence, and so much of my balance.

Everything was progressing nicely until 2013 when a second tumour was discovered, and this time I was old enough to know what it could mean. I was taken to Beaumont Hospital where the intricate skills of

Mr Darach Crimmons once again left us all feeling very thankful, and allowed me to resume my life.

Life is not perfect, of course, and even to this day I still have my problems, but when I do, my horse is my first port of call. I truly love those fascinating animals; I have now had four different horses, each one bringing me to another level, and teaching me so much, and I'm fortunate to have a great teacher, and friend, Janet Murray, who lives next door to me and is there 24/7 to help me. Thanks to all the support I've received, I have been involved in dressage, show jumping and cross country, and they have become such a big part of my life. In fact, I cannot image life without them.

Throughout my life, my family have been unbelievably supportive. I work full time with my brother, I recently moved into my own place (with lots of help from my folks), and I have my two horses out beside me, along with my donkey! I can honestly say that I have a great life now, and it's all down to my family and my horses who together have shown me how to live and enjoy life. They have all given me so much and brought so much light into my life, and I'm very grateful for it all. My hope now, is that by sharing my story, I can bring some hope, and some light, into somebody else's life.

Love Overcomes

Will Faulkner

She married young, a day off her twentieth birthday. Those were strange times, when women were forced from the civil service upon marriage. Imagine all the capable people the State turned away, swelling its senior ranks with hubris and testosterone for decades to come. Her career would be at home.

Far from the sunny meadows of childhood, a darkness stalked their honeymoon years. 'Her nerves are at her', people would whisper. Walls closed in as their circle grew smaller, one friendship strained after another, no bridge too sacred to burn. Demons preyed and angels defended but she was confused as to the difference, life's lens distorted.

Pregnancy brought fresh purpose, a new life to nurture, but joy was fleeting, blackened in post-natal shadow. When the buggy appeared without her, they said she wasn't well. As weeks turned to months, people wondered which hospital she was in. It must be Carlow.

The baby was too young to remember. An image of a doting mother leaning into his cot is where it all starts. They would be thick as thieves.

The child also loved his father dearly. He didn't understand why she packed their suitcases one cold day after school. The cavalry arrived, sending him to bed in hushed tones. A perch near the top of the stairs was his listening post, a path to be well-trodden.

Doctors often changed her medication. It worked for a while.

Her mother died horribly, the fiery agony of a rare infection. Grief left her trusting nobody, not even her cherished son. More months in hospital. She was smoking again. Time and tablets heal all wounds.

The boy was becoming a man, wise to cryptic conversation. *Schizoaffective disorder* came the reluctant answer. At least there was an explanation.

College produced an empty nest.

A lifetime went by, darkness a frequent visitor. Their time together was not how he had imagined at the altar. And yet, he stayed.

He was older. It wasn't unusual in those days. She was the most beautiful human being he'd ever met.

So how could she pawn off her engagement ring? And which new friend took the money? He struggled to separate person from illness, sustained by aching glimpses of the girl he once knew.

The chemical cocktail harmed her body, ushering challenges physical as well as mental.

He dreamed of retiring to Duncannon, to the endless beach and its gentle waves. On one side was a campsite of happy memories, inviting him to break free. On the other, an imposing army fort where his father once served. He would do his duty too.

The carer walks a lonely road. Hope springs eternal – and love overcomes.

Mary and Tim

Maria Brick

When I hear their tunes, it takes me back. I reminisce, remember. The melodies make me smile, shed a tear. Mary and Tim have both passed away, but my aunt and uncle's love lives on, in the music of their marriage.

When Mary died, five years after her Tim, I sat on her favourite chair, her throne beside the fire. The house, cold and empty, but still somehow warm with their presence. Opening the windows, I aligned her lace curtain with the utmost precision, almost hearing her voice. 'Is the net straight from the road Tim?' she would shout from the house, cocking her ear for his reply. The embroidered pleats, less rod-like, less rigid as she aged. Her fingers, stiff and swollen. No longer nimble enough to perfect straight lines.

On Fridays, she went to town, dolled up in her finery. Heading off around eleven. This her weekly outing. There she'd stroll, shopping till she dropped. Nattering with friends over silk-cut and tea. Around three, Tim prepared for her return, opening the door at each rev of an engine, watching each passing car. Arriving in the taxi like Cleopatra, Mary dismounted her chariot. Tim, jaunting down-path with a hop and a skip. Relieving her of the carrier bags, filled to the brim. 'How are you Mamie?' he'd ask, as if she'd been gone for years. Tim, so relieved to have her home again. Safe and snug, back in their nest.

They had left their life in Birmingham after the bombings in 1974. Tim's workplace colleagues, instead of friendly banter, gave him the snub, sending him to Coventry. Mary's local shops no longer rushed to serve her. Their happy lives changed. We all returned to Ireland. Home by the wild Atlantic Ocean, Kerry mountains and the sea.

My childhood memories of life in Birmingham fray and fade, but one snap-shot in time remains vivid. I clearly recall the record player. A square grey box with a heavy lid and velvety red interior. Its arm and needle, delicate and often prone to skidding. It commanded the room, awarded prime position. Its altar enhanced by Mary's red silk curtains, purchased somewhere posh.

One by one, Tim gently placed each 45 on the turntable. Lifting the disc with the palm of his hands, still greasy from fry-ups. The music would begin. Hits from the Capital Showband, Larry Cunningham, and Jim Reeves. I learnt to waltz, tutored by Tim on the tiny, lino floor. Mary, resplendent, ruby-lipped in Hepburn chic, polka dots and pearls, looked on fondly. Mouthing to me, the one, two, threes, while sipping a glass of Babycham.

Mary and Tim enriched my life with their humour and affection. Sound advice in spades, support, and endless cups of comfort. After they had both passed, I often strolled around their garden. Taking time to sit, reflect and think about the auld times. This sacred site where we drank gallons of tea, plucked spuds and spring onions, which Tim would say were, '... fit for the Queen of England'.

It was by chance I found it in the turf shed. A crumpled plastic carrier bag covered in beetles and dust. Buried and bulging under dark, black sods. Odd it was, that it lay disguised within the peat stack. I excavated the bundle, avoiding the army of insects. Raising it with an old broom, I sat the mystery down on the grass. In transit, its contents noised, scratching, and grating inside its confines. It brought my mind back to Uncle Pat, scuffing a thimble on a washboard, pretending to be Lonnie Donegan. His quiff in flight as he banged his foot, lost in the rhythms of skiffle.

My heart leapt. Strewn on the grass lay a pyramid of shiny black vinyl. These records, the soundtrack of my childhood, my little girl years. In disbelief, I plucked and dusted each one. Bugs and slugs dislodged, evicted. Like Carter in the Valley of the Kings, I had unearthed rare antiquities. A vinyl vault from a lost age raised not from sand, but a tomb of turf dust. I shifted the remaining sods, searching – yet no record player lay entombed to add to my treasure. It baffled me why Mary had tossed them into the darkness. The records told their story, chronicled their decades. It seemed the songs were banished, silenced. In the pain of her loss, she had cast them out, all life's music gone with Tim's passing.

In the broken remnants, I found their songs, Mary's, and Tim's favourites. The discs and their melodies mapped the flesh and bones of their marriage, their 50 years as one. I recall the tender looks exchanged between them as their songs played. Tim's adoration. Mary's shyness. The lyrics held their secret code as if written for them only.

Somewhere out there in the universe, they are both reunited. Waltzing high above the stars. The music of their love swirling them around, with those, one, two, threes. Mary and Tim. The greatest love.

You're Never Too Old,
and It's Never Too Late

Brid Stack

Self-belief is a funny thing. It goes through a journey as we navigate through the years. I looked at my young toddler son, Ógie, before writing this, and even in his short life I have seen him believe in himself and persevere to get what he wants. He falls down, he gets back up. He can't work something out, he'll ask for help and then claim the victory for himself at the end. We run races and when he crosses the line first, he exclaims, '*I'm* the best'.

Then we advance to school and meet our peers on a day-to-day basis. Over the years, these interactions have a deep-rooted influence on how we see the world and our position in it. I got involved in sport when I was seven and, through supportive parents and the enjoyment I got out of it, I stayed involved. I got involved in both individual and team sports and as the years rolled on, I understood the importance of the individual sports in my self-belief process, but I always gravitated towards the team environment. I love the idea of shipping the load together, each bringing our greatest attributes and working towards a common goal. Without realising it, team sports also prepared me for the world of work – respecting diverse personalities, discipline required to stay committed to task, and honesty of effort to play your role.

My self-belief was questioned many, many times throughout my sporting career but because of that, my resilience developed. Sport helped me to navigate that difficult school period where you question where you fit in, how to trust your gut and find your people. You make mistakes. I know, because I made plenty of them, but they all lead you to understand a greater sense of self. You don't have to have it all figured out. I still don't have it all figured out, but I trust my gut more and can now identify more quickly where I feel most comfortable and with whom.

I was so fortunate that I was part of a highly successful team; a team where every person wanted to make the people around them better. Be it becoming better footballers or better teammates, the self-belief we gave each other was phenomenal. Before one of the earlier All-Irelands, our manager, Eamonn Ryan, gave us all a copy of *The Story of the Geese*. For those that don't know, geese fly in a V formation. Those at the front lead while they can for a period of time, all the while being honked on from behind by the geese at the back of the V. They maintain the perfect V formation to not allow the wind to break momentum. Everyone stays connected. When they tire, the geese at the front drop back, and new geese lead the charge with those that have dropped back continuing to honk. I remember being on the way down to Cork with the team after that successful All-Ireland final when someone started to *Honk* and then the whole bus began to honk. It was magic. That team, and my journey through sport itself, gave me great belief in the power of the collective, and what I could contribute to it.

Fast-forward to the end of my career. I retired from intercounty sport at the age of thirty-two. When I got to that stage, I was so unbelievably content with what I had achieved with my best friends that I had complete peace with my retirement. However, an opportunity presented itself for me to take up a new sport, a new challenge, and play AFLW with the GWS Giants in Sydney, Australia. At thirty-four, my journey with self-belief had come full circle and I backed myself like my little Ógie does now when he sets his mind to something.

Was I scared? Yes.

Did I weigh up everything that could possibly go wrong? Yes.

Did everything work out the way I thought it would go? Absolutely not. It went Pete Tong for the first season. But life is for living and the greatest risk is not taking a risk. In August 2022, I lined up for my third season with the GWS Giants, on a family adventure with my husband and son. Now I truly believe.

You're never too old and it's never too late.

INDOMITABLE SPIRIT

James Saunders

'Hey Ógie', 'Pass it to Liam', 'Shoot'. It was great fun on the football pitch behind Gortnamona NS – well, not so much a pitch as a small hill with a goal at one end and two cones at the other. Our team won and, having scored more than twice as many goals as the next best player, the lads were laughing and calling me 'Salah'. Just as Tadhg hit the ball into the back of the net, the bell rang and we all lined up in our class groups.

The headmaster addressed the whole school, saying, 'We've had a good term and I hope you've all enjoyed it. I want to ask you to have a good Easter break and make sure to stay safe. Thank you.'

As we walked into the classroom, I was chatting with Ben and Darragh about the match, laughing, without a worry in the world. As soon as we sat down, our teacher told us that for the last two hours of school we could go outside again for PE. We didn't need to be told twice. We had a brilliant afternoon playing basketball, dodgeball and more. After that, the last few minutes of the day, and that term, were spent talking and relaxing.

Outside, after school, we said goodbye and, watching most of the others get into their parents' cars, I got on my bike and, stupidly as I now realise, set off without putting on my helmet. Luckily, I got home all right just in time to see Mum drive off to pick up my brother, Jack, from his school. Inside I followed my normal routine: pick up an orange from the fruit bowl, throw my bag down, run into the sitting room, collapse on the sofa, and turn on the television to watch a new episode of *The Flash* which had been recorded earlier in the day.

As soon as it ended I ran into the kitchen where Mum was making dinner. 'When's dinner goin' to be ready Mum?'

'It should be in about the next fifteen or 20 minutes' Mum responded. 'And tell me, are you looking forward to the holidays, James?'

'Ah yes, I am, it'll be nice to get a break, can you gimme a shout when dinner's ready?'

I grabbed my book, *It*, from my bag, went upstairs, fell on my bed, and started reading. After dinner I watched *The Late Late Show* before bed.

Teeth brushed and into bed, I read for another half an hour before going to sleep. What seemed like twenty or thirty minutes later I was awake again – but I wasn't in my bedroom! It was a strange, medical looking, room and, totally confused, I thought I was dreaming. Then I noticed Mum beside the bed, in an uncomfortable-looking armchair. I wanted to tell her what I believed was happening but it was hard to speak; my voice was very quiet, and hoarse.

Mum looked up, saw me trying to talk, and handed me a laminated sheet printed with the alphabet from A to Z and the numbers 0 to 9. Using it like a keyboard I could *type* with my right index finger. At the same time I realised my left arm was locked in a fully bent position. What was happening, where was I?

Now I started to feel sorry as Mum bent over, head in her hands, crying. 'James, thi-is is is Te-Temple Street. Y-you were, hit b-by a c-car,' she said, sniffling. I didn't know now whether I was dreaming or not, but I needed to find out. Using the laminated letterboard I asked several questions: where did it happen, when did it happen and who was driving? The answers came as a shock. It happened on the Tuesday before Easter, a car knocked me off my bike, it was close to home – and it had happened over three months ago! Since then I had been in an induced coma for a week and minimally conscious for the next ten weeks or so, although I could not, and still cannot, remember any of it.

I wanted to cry, but needed the bathroom even more and told Mum, expecting her to lower the side of the hospital bed. Instead, she picked up a bottle with a large opening, helped me pull down my pyjama bottoms, and indicated that this was where I would have to relieve myself. I didn't understand, I was confused, and shocked, and when I looked at Mum she gasped.

'Oh God, I didn't tell you, you-you're, well, you're not able to walk.'

'What? I'm, like, disabled?'

'Yes.'

I could feel a tear roll down my cheek as I typed, 'Anyway I should use this bottle now'.

After Mum had emptied the bottle in the bathroom, I continued to question her about my situation and what I had been doing in the hospital. I discovered that not only could I not talk, I couldn't walk, eat or even drink. How was I surviving without eating or drinking? She pointed to a tube, hanging out of my nose and taped to my cheek and explained how it was used for food, drink and various medicines. All the typing was making me, and my hand, tired, so I had to rest, but continued to show my shock by using facial expressions.

With my hand rested, I was back asking questions, I wanted to know whether all the limitations were permanent or not. Mum told me, 'The doctors said a lot of it would probably stay for the foreseeable future, but if we work hard maybe, just maybe, we'll come through'. Were my Dad and my brother at home? Yes, they were. Who was here in Temple Street with me? There was Ronan and Aisling, both of whom I got to know well, and she told me my doctor was doing a wonderful job.

In due course, it was time for physio and this is when I really found out what my physical disabilities were. On the way I had met Temple Street's head porter and Mum told him about my loss of memory. She later told me that he was the encapsulation of the Temple Street spirit, and how he helped all the patients and their families through hospital.

Lying in bed that night I was totally confused and unsure of myself, my whole world had been turned upside down. It then dawned on me that during the time I had been 'out of it', the new *Avengers* movie I'd been looking forward to would have been released. I asked Mum if I could watch all the Marvel movies in order, finishing with the new *Avengers* and, in her usual caring voice, she said, 'I'd love to watch them with you'.

The tough hospital routine continued for several days before I heard they had to change the naso-gastric tube in my nose. This sounded okay until I realised that something in your nose only has one way in and one way out. I thought about begging the nurses to let it be, but I knew as well as they did that this was not going to happen. Mum was sitting beside me holding my hand as the nurse pulled the tube out of my nose. It was painless and I felt like cheering, until I remembered that another one had to go in. I took Mum's hand again and as I looked at her in fear, she looked back with a sympathetic, and caring, expression on her face. It made me feel a little better, but the nurse could not wait much longer; she told me how sorry she was as she inserted the tube in my left nostril and started pushing. I was choking for air as the pain increased and I felt as if someone had started pushing a pencil up my nose. The worst thing was that the pain continued for far too many moments until the nurse had finished and let go. I almost cursed at her before realising how unreasonable that would be.

For the next month, most days were much the same: a mix of physio, speech and language therapy, and occupational therapy, and endless hours in bed. Every few weeks I would have the joy of another naso-gastric tube fitted, but nothing particularly out of the ordinary. That was until one day my doctor said he would have to give me a Botox injection and put my arm into serial casting to bring it back to its rightful position. It all sounded merry and bright until I learned how painful the process would be.

I decided this was another case of 'no pain no gain', and was determined to just face it. A few days later it was time, and I was *not* looking forward to it, but with the irritation of having my arm contracted, I was ready to face it. When the doctor came in, I could see how sorry he was about the pain he was going to inflict on me and, surprisingly, knowing he was not enjoying it made me feel a little better.

Sitting beside the bed, he produced a very large needle on the end of which was a large capsule containing clear liquid, which I could only assume was Botox. I tried to brace myself but nothing could have prepared me for the agony that came once he started to push the end of the needle sending the Botox into my bicep. Although the pain was excruciating I was delighted to find my arm slightly looser and freer, but then it was time to start the serial casting.

A man I'd never met before came to put on the cast, which we had previously been decided would be red. He started by painfully pulling my arm down before seeing the pain I was in, and easing off a little into a less painful, but still uncomfortable, position. With the cast in place, he left it to set.

Before I knew it, it was October – I could barely believe that in a few days I would be thirteen years old! I was looking forward to the celebration, but disappointed it was going to be spent in hospital, so different to previous birthdays. Come the day, I was a little bit excited, but unfortunately more disappointed at all the negatives. When Mum came in and wished me happy birthday she looked as if she had more exciting plans, though I couldn't imagine what. Later that morning we went down to the front desk where the head porter smiled and wished me the happiest of birthdays and asked if I was looking forward to seeing all my family. I was totally confused as he turned to Mum and asked whether she had told me or not. Mum covered her mouth and gasped before saying she had forgotten to tell me the whole family were coming today to celebrate. I was delighted, it meant I'd be able to do something to mark the occasion.

As the family arrived, they brought food, cards, presents and love, and I was thrilled that having progressed noticeably since getting my memory back, I was able to eat some of the food! It was great to catch up with some family members I hadn't seen in God knows how long and when they had to say goodbye a few hours later, I returned to my room, very happy with the day I'd just had.

My parents had a ramp installed outside our front door for my wheelchair, and a hospital bed was put in my bedroom so, a week later, I was able to go home for the weekend, thanks to a ride in a 'Bumbleance'. The food in Temple Street was fine but nothing could compare with Mum's brilliant cooking, and I enjoyed every single mouthful.

Later that month came Halloween, and while I wouldn't normally dress up, because times had been so grim I decided I would. Life was hard enough for them, so for the sake of the little kids I didn't want anything too scary, or ugly, so, to show some hope, and reflect the indomitable spirit we were all developing, I decided to go as Rocky Balboa. The little party was in the physio gym, where everyone was dressed up, and I arranged with Mum for her to play 'Eye of the Tiger' when I went in. There were cheers and claps and we had a brilliant night full of games, laughs and fun – I even won an award for best costume!

After several more days of therapy, from physio to speech and language, to occupational therapy and more it was finally time to leave Temple Street once and for all. Mum and I were very emotional as we said our goodbyes to everyone who had worked with me, and helped me, before we left the hospital for the last time.

During two stays in the National Rehabilitation Hospital, where I got two awards for my work, that indomitable spirit was back – with a lot of hard work and determination – and resulted in me now being able to walk, talk, eat and drink on my own. And I haven't stopped yet!

Following my successful recovery, I want everyone to remember:

If your mind can conceive it,
and your heart can believe it,
then you can achieve it.

SPOT – ALIAS GRAND MORN

Tony Gately

For me in the mid-1960s, Sunday mornings in leafy Monkstown were dictated by solemn prayer at high mass with my parents, followed by the ritual polishing of brass and whitewashing of spats for my brother's Scottish piper's uniform, in preparation for his performance later that day in the People's Park, Dun Laoghaire. He always gave me a half crown for my toil and I was always so grateful to have this cash flow, even at the young age of eight.

My earliest memories of Dun Laoghaire are of imperial monuments, Teddy's Ice-Cream, the long piers, the ferry boats and the boat train, Johnny Carr's playground, Johnson, Mooney and O'Brien's Café, Woolworths, the Pawn Office, lovely sandy beaches and plenty of summer sunshine.

Despite the beauty of their surroundings the good people of South Dublin needed a distraction every now and then, and they found it in the battle of the mongrels' race. This took place once a month at one side of TEK's pitch which was named after the local dairy, due to the fact that the team had a lot of milk men playing for TEK soccer club at that time. The course consisted of one length of the football pitch with traps at the starting end, and an upturned bicycle at the far end just past the finishing line. The 'hare' – which I always suspected was some child's unloved teddy bear – was attached to a wire, which was magically connected to the bicycle.

The dogs would eye up each other before the race, and the bookies would eye up the canine competitors, giving odds for each participant. Now, in general, the long-legged dogs were favourites, with the known unknowns a little further out in the betting. What bookmaker Terry Rogers couldn't price for, however, was the possibility of a sting, especially one orchestrated by an eight-year-old boy.

We felt that our dog, Spot, was the ideal candidate to participate in this unusual enterprise. He was about three years old, which we figured was the prime age to start an athletic career, so my Dad gave him the racing name, *Grand Morn*. He was a beautiful brown and white collie whom our family loved very much. But there was stiff competition in these races, and it came in the form of German shepherds, bulldogs, beagles, pugs, poodles, boxers, Yorkshire terriers, terrier crosses, and indeed some cross terriers. Added to these were some breeds and half breeds that even if God himself was a veterinarian, he wouldn't have been able to identify.

Cadburys were great employers in Dublin, but little did they realise when they were founded in the East Wall of Dublin in 1932, that someday their confectionery would influence the outcome of a sporting occasion.

Spot – or should I say *Grand Morn* – loved chocolate, and occasionally, when he hadn't done so well in his last few outings, I would give him a sniff of this heavenly sweet just before he was led into the traps. Mister O'Connor of Monkstown would ensure all dogs were safely secured, the 'hare' would suddenly appear on a wire between the enclosures – powered by two very strong men who peddled the upside-down bicycle – and Mr O'Connor would release the trapdoors.

The hairy warriors would leap out of their temporary dark incarnation in search of glory in a scene the makers of *Braveheart* would have been proud of. The runners would bump and swagger and fall as they chased the 'hare', lacking some of the elegance of a modern-day greyhound race, but still determined to get their teeth into that Woolworths teddy bear. Thanks to Cadburys, *Grand Morn* overtook the 'hare' at least twice as he had a different goal in mind, and his prize came in the shape of a silver foil and blue wrapper.

I guess this was the precursor of, not an illegal, but perhaps an immoral, use of a substance in sport. I don't think my Dad was ever aware of my little plot to divert the course of sporting justice, but he was definitely grateful for his winnings on those fine summer grand morns in Monkstown.

THE MAGNIFICENT SEVEN

Alan Corcoran

There are some who believe you should never meet your heroes, as the reality may be somewhat different to your perception. So, what happens when you do eventually meet people whom you have admired over the years? Does it change your views, or does it strengthen your respect for them?

As a professional broadcaster for over thirty years working for RTÉ and for South East Radio, I have met, and interviewed, hundreds of people from all walks of life. Every so often, however, an added bonus is that I get to meet people I have admired for the impact they have made in their chosen field, so let me take you on a short journey of my impressions of some of the people I have met – my *Magnificent Seven*.

As a young student in the CBS Wexford, the first album my friend and I bought was *Live at San Quentin* and I became hooked on the music and the legend of the *man in black*, Johnny Cash. His story telling and his songwriting just blew me away.

Working for RTÉ in 1993, I got a call from TV producer Ian McGarry asking me to host a series of TV Concerts at the Olympia in Dublin. Headlining one of them was Johnny Cash and I met him in the theatre during the day before the concert. It is a meeting I will never forget; a warm handshake, a big smile, and a genuine interest in what radio was like in Ireland. He was cordial, welcoming, and one of the humblest men I ever met. I introduced him on stage and as he passed me, he said, 'Al, I'm going on to do the show, after Folsom Prison Blues, I'll finish, you go on and thank the band, and if they like me I'll come back on. If they don't, you're on your own!'

He laughed, went on the stage and was brilliant. My final memory was of a limo arriving to take him off for a special recording with U2. To this day that memory of meeting Johnny Cash stands out.

As broadcasters, we all have people who influence us in our careers. Mine include Larry Gogan, Vincent Browne, and, of course, Gay Byrne, but my biggest influence was Terry Wogan. He won over audiences in Great Britain at a time when being Irish was not a major advantage. It was a time of great uncertainty yet Terry broke the mould with his warmth and professionalism.

In 1999 I was sent to Birmingham to cover the Eurovision Song Contest and my boss and mentor Bill O'Donovan asked me if I would like to interview Terry, who was covering the event for the BBC. I jumped at the opportunity and visited Terry at his hotel; he was everything I hoped he would be, and more. We sat and chatted for ages and, in a busy schedule for him, as I produced the recorder for our interview he waved his hand and said, 'No not a portable recorder Alan! Come to the BBC studios and we'll record it there'. It remains one of the most memorable interviews of my broadcasting life. Terry was a legend and I will never forget his kindness.

Bill O'Donovan came to me on another occasion to tell me, 'There's a new kid on the comedy block called Brendan O'Carroll. He's going to be a big star but he hasn't done a radio interview yet and I'd like you to do one'. We clicked instantly, here was a warm hearted and very, very funny guy, driven by a belief in himself. It was clear to me he was going to be a star. He very quickly went on to appear regularly on *The Late Late Show* and to get his own radio feature, *Mrs Brown's Boys*, leading eventually to the TV show and movie. I recorded a piece with him for RTÉ *Nationwide* in his home, and whenever he is in my native Wexford, we meet up. For all his success, he has never forgotten his roots.

Blues man Don Baker and I became great friends in the early nineties. He is one of the top five harmonica players in the world, and an amazing guy in so many ways, but he always harboured a desire to be an actor. One time when he was performing in Wexford he popped up for dinner in our house, and said he was expecting some big news and a few days later he rang to say he had been cast as Joe McAndrew in the movie *In the Name of the Father*. Don never forgot our friendship and invited my wife, Ann Marie, and me to the movie launch where we were thrilled to meet Daniel Day Lewis, Pete Postlethwaite and other members of the cast, as well as some of the original members of the Guildford four.

Sport has always played a huge part in my life, especially hurling and soccer. The Leeds United team of the seventies was one of the most iconic teams of that decade, and Johnny Giles was one of the focal points of that team. I have met him on many occasions but the first meeting was special as we clicked and instead of your standard football interview it became a heartfelt chat. It was a real insight into one of the greatest footballers ever to wear the green jersey for Ireland. Some of his family live in Wexford, and an interesting footnote is that my son found himself in opposition to Johnny's grandson in a recent soccer match. Johnny Giles was, and is, everything I hoped he would be.

There is no question about my proudest moment as a broadcaster. It happened when I was given the opportunity of interviewing President Mary Robinson in Áras an Uachtaráin. It took weeks to get permission, but, as the grandson of one of the men who fought with Michael Collins and then went on to become one of the first members of An Garda Síochána, interviewing the President, surrounded by portraits of former Presidents, was a real privilege and a memory I cherish and treasure.

Adorning one of the walls in on our kitchen is a poster for *The Quiet Man*, my favourite movie of all time. Maureen O'Hara co-starred with

John Wayne and it was like a dream come true when I met and interviewed this Hollywood legend. She arrived at a hotel in Glengarriff for the interview, with her daughter, in a chauffeur driven limousine and we met her, as we had been advised to, with chocolates and a special bouquet of flowers.

I didn't know what to expect. Would she be aloof? Would she be distant? She was none of these, she was just brilliant. One of the most powerful women I have ever met, she exuded absolute confidence, but also warmth and respect. Even as she rolled off the names of the Hollywood greats she had worked with, you could sense that she never lost her love of family or her native Ireland.

As a broadcaster I am very lucky that my Magnificent Seven made so many dreams come true for me, but what struck me most, is that for all their fame and status, behind the glitz and the glamour, they were all just normal people.

CHERNOBYL HEART

Adi Roche

The tragedy of Chernobyl may seem like a historic event to many; there may even be an impression that 37 years on it no longer poses a threat to the world, but the reality is very, very different. Chernobyl is not something from the past; Chernobyl is, sadly, forever. The impact of that single shocking nuclear accident can never be undone; its radioactive footprint is embedded in our world forever as we cannot undo the genetic impact.

On that fateful day of the accident, 26 April 1986, Chernobyl entered the history of language, the history of disasters and the history of the world with a terrible and frightening force.

In most tragedies it is children who pay the highest price and when it comes to radiation it's no different, with their small bodies absorbing adult doses, and those who were children themselves in 1986 are now parents and grandparents, and we see what is referred to as 'Chernobyl Lineage', where the effects cross into the third generation.

The heart was quickly identified as being seriously damaged by Chernobyl, most particularly the tiny hearts of little babies. The heart is a powerful organ in the body, the symbol of the heart speaks of love and life to all of us. How terrible that the heart has been so damaged by a condition now known as 'Chernobyl Heart'. But! This is not meant to be a sad story. In fact, it's not! It's about the power of intervention, the power of love and the power of hope and how anything is possible once you belive in the power of the possible.

While walking through a children's hospital in Southern Belarus during the early nineties, I was stopped in my tracks when a small boy shouted: 'Please take me to your country, I will die if you leave me here.' I was stunned to learn about all the children suffering from an untreatable condition the local surgeons called 'Chernobyl Heart'. We were told by a doctor, 'This small boy cannot live with this condition, but he can die with it ... without treatment.' We managed to airlift not just nine-year-old Vitaly, who had shouted out to save his life, but three other children, each suffering from the same untreated condition. Thanks to the experts at both the Mercy Hospital in Cork and Crumlin Hospital in Dublin, the lives of three of those children were saved. Sadly, eight-year-old Evgeniya died, but in her name we subsequently developed a world-class cardiac programme in both Belarus and Ukraine which continues to save the lives of thousands of babies and small children today.

I remember standing in a Ukrainian hospital many years later having a heated discussion with local doctors about a little boy called Edik who suffered from 'Chernobyl Heart'. At seven months old he suffered from three separate heart defects. Emaciated and losing muscle, he was starving to death in spite of the loving attentions of his mother and grandmother. For little Edik, feeding was like running a marathon: all the calories he took into his body went to feed his respiratory and heart muscles, which were working double time to compensate for holes in his heart that sent too much blood to his lungs, and not enough to his small body.

The local doctors hadn't the equipment, or the skills, to save him and said, sadly, 'We will have to let him die ... take him home to die.' We said our surgeons wanted to try to save him – that we would do all we could to save him, explaining that we would fight for his little life to his last breath. We wore them down and eventually our surgeons took Erik to theatre where they performed life-saving surgery on him.

I was there in the operating theatre with Dr Novick, our chief cardiac surgeon from America. I can still remember the moment when they stopped little Edik's heart and the moment before the bypass machine kicked in. It felt like time stood still ... the only sound was the spluttering of the bypass machine as it kicked in ... I remember how Dr Novick held Edik's tiny, troubled, heart in his huge hand as he delicately repaired it, and ... *time* stood still ... I witnessed a miracle that day. Edik lived, and today he is a bright and energetic young boy!

His story is about miracles, but it is also about perseverance ... not giving up ... believing that with effort and vision ... miracles can happen ... I believe in miracles! Hope is transformative. Hope is fantastic. We always say one heart at a time! Breath by breath ... our hope and theirs! These children put their hope and their hearts in our hands. One by one we try together to make a miracle happen!

This programme not only saves the lives of babies and children but it does side-by-side training and teaching as an inbuilt component, to ensure sustainability. This programme is still in operation despite the invasion and the war in Ukraine!

There is an old Irish saying that describes how our organisation thinks, '*Is ar scath a chéile a mhaireann na daoine*'. We truly live in the shadow of each other. That closeness, that intimacy is the same for us all – connected – part of the same web of life. That's what makes us truly human – full of love for each other and we astonish ourselves at times at how much we can feel and do, to help even the stranger – the child in Syria, the man in Afghanistan, the woman in Yemen.

Thank God, our hearts are big, generous and capable of so much giving and sharing. Of being able to love. Every child deserves to have hope! Thanks to kind and generous people we can help restore lost and stolen childhoods to children, in Ireland and around the world. We fight for every life. Heartbeat by heartbeat! Breath by breath! For we believe that nothing is more precious in life than life itself.

The stories of Vitaly and Edik led us to rediscover our hope, we found our hearts, and we rose once again, reaching out with joy and resolve, and with the help and hope and heart of the people of Ireland we succeeded, for ourselves and our dear children in Belarus and Ukraine. For hope drives out all fear, binding us together, driving us to persevere against the odds. Hope conquers despair and restores our faith and confidence in ourselves, and the power of the ordinary citizen to find the strength and vision to see a better world. For hope is indeed, the most enabling gift of all!

Through the work of Make-A-Wish and other charities we are being offered the wonderful privilege of saving or improving the life of another human being. Giving our time, our energy, our money, our concern for the sake of another person, someone we don't know – that indeed is true love, true Christianity in practice, and the *return profit* of peace and happiness in our lives is beyond our wildest dreams.

Sinéad

Aidee Lyons

Sinéad was a joy, and a lovely, lively, lucky little girl, from the moment, she was born. Nothing ever fazed her. She met every challenge, every obstacle, head on. She lived and loved every minute of every day.

Her love of adventure, and her degree in IT, took her to the USA in 2006, where she settled in Boston. She loved the work, the weather, and the attention that being tall, blonde and Irish brought her.

One of her, and our, very proudest moments, and there were many, was when, after being there four years, she became an American citizen. My sister Fiona and her partner David flew down from Canada to join us in the civic centre in Boston, where we clapped and cheered as hundreds of new citizens shouted out the pledge of allegiance to their new country.

The great thing about becoming a US citizen was that it meant Sinéad could now travel freely, and she did. She got a car and regularly drove up to meet her cousins in Canada. And, as well as us going there, she could now come home regularly. She loved Ireland, loved meeting up with everyone and being part of all the family events. Until Covid struck, of course.

On one occasion, when Sinéad was travelling home, she had a five-hour layover in Chicago, which she was dreading. When she eventually arrived I'd expected her to be exhausted, but not a bit of it. As she was queueing for coffee and a sandwich in the airport in the US, she got chatting to a nice guy, who it turned out, happened to be the pilot. Not alone did he take her out for a slap-up meal, but he bumped her up to first class. We laughed: it could only happen to Sinéad.

In March 2021, Sinéad, having been away for a week with her boyfriend Steve, went to collect her beautiful German Shepherd, Flossie, from kennels in New Hampshire, three hours away. The kennels belonged to an old friend and neighbour of hers, so she knew Flossie would be well looked after, making the long journey well worth the effort.

It was a beautiful day with blue skies, and a beautiful place with a white lake nestled in the mountains, and it was reasonably warm for March. She couldn't resist taking Flossie for a walk, playing ball, and chasing each other across the frozen lake.

You cannot imagine the horror, the terror, of hearing that your daughter, sister, niece, cousin, or loved one, is missing. In a foreign country, in the mountains, in the middle of a pandemic. Every horror film, every murder story, every horrible thing you have ever heard runs in a continuous, never-ending loop, through your mind.

It's very hard to find anything hopeful, or inspirational in this story, but there was. Because people are unbelievable and unstoppable. Our daughter, our son-in-law, our family, friends, friends of family, family of friends, neighbours, colleagues, Facebook, Aer Lingus crew, officials, people in New Hampshire, total strangers. They all stepped up, reached out, and surrounded us with love, support, and kindness.

And most of all Kempes, the detective assigned to find Sinéad and Flossie – he, and all of the officers in the State Police and the Fish and Game Department. We were awed by their kindness, their dedication, and their determination to help us to find them. They worked day and night, they dived into a freezing lake, and they found them. And we brought them home.

My beautiful daughter Sinéad, aged forty-two, and her beautiful two-year-old German Shepherd, Flossie, are gone. There are no words to describe their loss. But because of Detective Kempes and all those people who helped us find them, we know that they died tragically, accidentally, on a beautiful day, on a beautiful frozen lake, while dancing together.

May they rest in peace.

The Leitrim Triplets and the Country Doctor

John Dorman

Some time ago a young Leitrim woman was in Sligo visiting her sister when she unexpectedly went into labour. Her sister called her GP, my father, who directed her to Garden Hill Nursing Home where he helped deliver three beautiful babies, six weeks early.

As the nursing home had no incubator, they were tucked up in three wicker baskets, put into the back of his car, and with no time to lose, driven quickly to Sligo General Hospital. Mary, Paddy Joe and Peter Daly spent the next three months in an incubator, initially in Sligo, then Manorhamilton, before returning to their Leitrim cottage as local celebrities. This happy occasion became the impetus for Garden Hill to acquire an incubator, something which he had been canvassing for.

My dad had never seen *his* triplets since that time, but one day his granddaughter recounted a story she had heard in the news about triplets, which reminded him of an invitation he had received to the twenty-first birthday party for the first and only triplets he delivered during his working life. He asked my sister and I to go on a mission to find these triplets; he didn't think it was too long ago, and he regretted that he had been too busy at the time to attend.

Now, at ninety-four, with a bit more time on his hands, he was determined to meet them. We had no names, addresses or contact details, except for a rough idea of the area in Leitrim. 'We'll go to Drumkeeran and ask in McPadden's shop. She was a patient of mine, she'll know', he suggested confidently. So, in the middle of January we headed off into the depths of Leitrim in search of the lost triplets, passing along Leitrim's winding roads over rolling drumlins patterned with small fields, many overshadowed by dark looming pine forests. Every so often he would point out a farm or building and recount an incident or story from his days doing house calls.

'See that church there?', he said, pointing at a small church sitting up above a bend on the road, '... I once bought a fine mare from the parish priest there. A week later he rang me up and asked if he could buy it back, explaining that he was heartbroken without it, so of course I returned her.'

Sadly, over time, many of the people and patients he once knew had died and in the tiny village of Drumkeeran many of the old shops too were gone, including McPadden's. We enquired at the local neon-lit supermarket for triplets aged about 25 or 30. Alas, we drew a blank until a customer walked in and overheard us.

'I know of triplets who had their fiftieth birthday some time ago. If you wish I can show you where one lives out the road a bit?'

Their age seemed improbable to us but as it was the only lead we had, we followed her out the road to a tidy farm where we met a few young lads and their dad, Paddy Joe. 'It's a long shot but by any chance were you born in Sligo?' we asked a little awkwardly, '... as we are trying to trace triplets our Dad helped deliver in Sligo some time ago.' 'Would that be Dr Dorman?', he asked, pointing at the older man in the car with some incredulity. 'Yes, we were born in Sligo and he was the doctor who delivered us!'

This reunion was a magical moment with Paddy Joe leaning in the car window, holding my Dad's hand, bridging over a half century of time. The day became more special when we went further into Leitrim, in convoy, to meet his sister Mary and her husband and daughter. Again, greeted warmly, we were invited in for tea and offered that very special hospitality so typical in rural Ireland.

Two months later Peter returned from England for the triplets' sixtieth birthday party where Dr Michael, sitting beside one of his oldest Leitrim patients, Mary Flynn, was the guest of honour. The reunion was now complete. Dad was so happy and comfortable to be among the kind of people he gave so much to and who, in return, gave him so much over his 60 years in practice as a GP in the west of Ireland, in particular the Sligo and Leitrim people, for whom he holds so much affection.

Emotions may have been running high the following day in Croke Park when Leitrim played Derry, but the tears were only of joy on that night at Drumkeeran's big reunion between the triplets and the country doctor.

My Mum, the love of his life, who had died just two years earlier, would have so enjoyed this coming together. Life offers some wonderful moments of surprise, happiness and joy.

BE THE BEST YOU

Antonia Hendron

When you are young you feel as though you can accomplish anything, conquer the world, live your dreams. In truth, you can – at any age; if you want it, take it, it's all there for you. Just be aware that while you are in your youth, whilst it's within your grasp, it can so easily slip away because if you don't believe you can do it, it doesn't believe in you, so grab it while you can.

The oldest child is always on the clock, and I should know, I am one. There are special privileges that are granted, but the pressure to live up to expectation is always there. It's a poisoned chalice for the simple reason that while it can push you forward, it can also leave you stifled.

So, if you are the oldest kid, go easy on yourself, and remember to go with the flow as there is no one in your way. Relax. Being the oldest child can help you forge relationships with people, fight your own battles, make your own way, and even become a boss, because no one came before you.

You have to be fearless and beat a path less travelled. Revel in it. It means you are writing your own story, you own history, and there is no comparative version of you that has gone before. You are supremely you, and if you own it, if you embrace you for all that you are, flaws and all, then you will have something so powerful that nothing can stop you becoming whatever you want to be in life.

Why am I telling you this? Because as a community leader in my field I want to empower you to follow your goals and to use the hand you have been dealt to the best of your advantage. Regardless of family position, class, gender, race or creed, if you believe in you, you're already ahead of the pack, and I promise you there are rewards to follow.

When I was elected as president of The Society of the Irish Motor Industry in 2022 I was so proud and grateful to be in a position to help galvanise changes in the transition of the motor industry.

As Managing Director of the M50 Truck and Van Centre for the previous five years, I felt energised by the maelstrom of change that was around me and, as a woman in what is traditionally a male-dominated industry, felt that my unique position gave an exciting energy to initiatives in our dynamic motor industry. It's a position I have always respected, and one I certainly didn't take for granted when I occupied it.

When I think of leading by example for my own children, Sophia and Tom, I want them to understand that at a sensitive age, anything is possible, and achievable, when it is underpinned by belief, grit and determination.

If I was taught anything by my parents, and if I was to proffer any advice to younger people, it is these core values that I believe have helped me get to where I am today.

Though a lot of obstacles and roadblocks will inevitably stand in your way, it is that fastidious belief in you that will take you places and if, through all the murky waters, you can hold tight to that righteous truth in yourself, even when all others would try your intention, you will end up exactly where you're supposed to be.

OLYMPIC DREAMS

Lord Clifton Wrottesley

I am often asked to re-live those crazy few hours in Salt Lake City back in 2002 that would define so much of the rest of my life. But for a slight mistake made on the twelfth corner of my second run down the Park City skeleton track, the tricolour would have incredibly been flying during a Winter Olympic medal ceremony. Sadly, it was not to be, but it was certainly a wild ride, getting there, being there and since.

I missed a bronze medal by 0.42 of a second, a razor-thin margin, but in the Olympics there are no prizes for coming fourth, except maybe a pewter medal from the Lord Mayor of Dublin. That one tiny mistake on corner twelve was the difference between third and fourth. However, it still remains the best result Ireland has achieved at the Winter Olympics. But as with all records, it's there to be broken, so I guess for now, I'll stay as one of Ireland's most infamous losers, a mantle I wear with pride!

But we will get to that. Firstly, a brief biography. Born in Lower Hatch Street (you couldn't make it up!), Dublin in 1968, I spent the first couple of years of my life at Newtown House, outside Abbeyknockmoy in rural

Galway, where my father The Hon Richard Wrottesley, a former British army soldier, had a pig farm.

As a prospective National Service officer, my father attended Mons Officer Cadet School with the renowned adventurer, Ranulph Fiennes. Together they decided to visit a local girls' boarding school one night, and were apprehended 70 feet up the west wing looking, as they claimed, for a lesser spotted newt, or some such. The Bursar called them down from the wall, at which point my father gave him a gentle fist bump to his nose and tried to make good his escape.

Unfortunately, they were later separately apprehended by the police, who remarked that they rather gave themselves away, being dressed in their Army PT kit. Back at Mons, father got thrown out, Ranulph received fifty-six days 'restrictions of privileges', a record that still stands to this day. After that, my father joined the Parachute Regiment as a trooper, a private soldier, and was later commissioned as an officer.

After a short stint in the Army, he retired to motor racing and then tried his hand at winter sports, spending two to three months of every winter holed up in the Swiss Alps, plying his trade. I guess that's where my love of the mountains, speed, snow and ice sports began. You could say it was in the genes.

Everything changed on a November night in 1970 when my father, returning from Dublin Airport, died when his Jaguar E-type crashed into Ballinamore Bridge, less than twenty miles from home. He didn't leave a will, so my mother fled to Spain where she could escape the inevitable scrutiny of a disapproving family, the cost of living was cheaper, and the climate a little more agreeable. Accidents, whether happy or otherwise, always throw up challenges, but whatever you face in life, how you respond is what defines you as a person.

When my grandfather died, his peerage came to me at the tender age of nine, along with some money to pay for my education. By this time my grandmother was fed up with me speaking English to her in a Spanish accent, so we went to live with her in the UK.

With the peerage came the right to sit in the House of Lords and when I came of age at 21, I made a maiden speech in the House. However, a few years later, Tony Blair trimmed the number of sitting Lords and I was one of those to have my seat removed, although I may have a go at being elected sometime in the not too distant future.

My sporting career is more of a *happy accident*, as my talent and skill as a slider was only discovered by a desire to find out more about my father. In my early twenties, I went to the Swiss Alps where my father's exploits on, and more often off, the fabled Cresta Run in St Moritz were the stuff of legend.

My dad died when I was only two, so obviously I didn't remember him, and what I knew about him came from my grandmother. My mother never talked about him. I thought that one way of getting to know my father better, and understand what made him tick, was to visit some of the places he had been to. And loved. And I knew St Moritz was close to his heart. Going there was a way to connect with him, it was like a pilgrimage to see what he was all about. In their twenties I suppose everyone is trying to find some meaning in life, and I just went there to discover what he got up to.

You could say it was a pretty successful mission. Going to St Moritz was the start of the rest of my life, meeting my wife and raising a family, forging a career around the Cresta, and going to the Olympics.

The Cresta Run is a natural skeleton racing track in the Swiss resort, where sliders go down head-first on a track that drops 157 metres in three-quarters of a mile. I've had a pretty successful career on the Run, as we call it, winning the Grand National (the second oldest winter sports trophy in the world) a record fifteen times. And I'm still competing now, in my fifties, although younger athletes are snapping at my heels. There's an inevitability in having to hand over the mantle, but keeping myself in some sort of shape has helped extend my career significantly.

My consistency on the Cresta comes from my time working at the tobogganing club in St Moritz after leaving the army. I was trying to figure out what to do with the rest of my life and one morning in the shower, where I do my best thinking, I had an idea of staying in St Moritz and working at the club. So, I ended up doing all the jobs nobody else wanted to do, but managed almost 150 runs that season, ten times what I would normally have managed. Practice makes perfect …

Over three months, I got a season of experience on the Cresta and by the end of the 1995/96 season, I was a regular in the top ten. My exploits caught the attention of Tony Wallington, Performance Director of the British bobsleigh team, who head-hunted me for the 1998 Olympics. Tony thought I had a good feel for the ice, but I ran out of talent where the bob was concerned. I turned it over three times in a row on the easiest track in the world, so that was me finished with bobsleigh.

Fate would intervene, however, when the International Olympic Committee added skeleton, essentially a refined version of the Cresta Run, to the 2002 Games. Another *happy accident*! I decided I'd regret it for the rest of my life if I didn't give it a go and, as some might suggest, rather foolishly set aside a place at Imperial College Business School to pursue the dream of competing at the Olympics.

I put together a plan, with the goal of the Games at the pinnacle, and set achievable goals along the way, each one making the eventual stretch goal of a top ten placing seem achievable.

A strength and conditioning programme and fitness regime was developed with the help of Simon Timson, then Performance Director of British Skeleton and now part of Manchester City's brains trust. However, with the British team being a closed-shop, I set about putting together my own – and slid for Ireland.

I recruited Irish Canadian slider Tim Cassin as a team-mate and went through rigorous training at his home track in Calgary, where I finished twenty first in the World Championships that same season. It was the first step to reaching the Olympics, and suggested it was no pipe dream.

But most on the circuit saw me as nothing more than an oddity. I was a curiosity when I started off. Nobody took me too seriously, I was probably seen as the playboy from St Moritz, hijacking their sport where they were all super professional and had been at it for years.

I took advantage of that anonymity, banking up to sixty runs at the Olympic skeleton track in Park City the year before the Games, because nobody saw me as a threat. I also took advantage of a nascent concept, a point of view film of myself going down the track, making half a dozen copies and trading them with my mates, who were also my competitors, in return for coaching tips and track information.

The VHS tapes of the track were my currency on the circuit. Competitors all helped each other out then, there was more of a fraternal feel. So, I was able to trade in tapes and get hints and tips from other competitors. It's a lot different these days, much more money involved, much more professional, the secrets guarded more closely, held much closer to one's chest.

Ironically, the three competitors who bumped me out of the medals were the three who were most helpful to me on the circuit – Jimmy Shea, Martin Rett and Gregor Stähli. They were my mates, still my mates, and I would have felt terrible had I stolen a medal away from any of them. But I almost did. By the end of the final training run I was no longer an oddity, but firmly a viable medal contender, having finished fourth and seventh in two of my training runs. Suddenly, I was on everyone's radar.

There was an immediate backlash. The American team lodged a spurious objection based on a custom-made helmet we'd developed. The objection was rejected, though the experience did rattle me a bit. Reflecting on it at the time, I concluded that the only reason they'd bothered to lodge a complaint was because they now saw me as a serious contender, a threat to their own ambitions. So, I turned a potentially unsettling experience into a positive, turning the nerves and apprehension into aggression, wanting to show them that I was worthy of that fear they apparently felt about me.

Next morning, I hurtled down the track I'd got to know so well in a time of 51.07, third fastest of the first run. Not really believing I'd get myself into medal contention, I set my heart on a top six finish, an Olympic Diploma. In training, I was getting into the top ten, so had a vague idea we might be in touching distance, but no idea we would be in line for a medal.

It was good in one way not having any real expectations, but in another way, it wasn't, because I was totally unprepared for being in medal contention. While everyone was saying 'Who the hell is that?' after my first run, I was going, 'What the hell, I'm in third!' Psychologically, I wasn't properly prepared for it. Maybe if I was, I could have replicated my first run, but the rest is history.

In the second run, I made a small mistake in the entrance of corner twelve, and that was the difference between winning a medal and not. But finishing fourth was the right result. Jimmy, Martin and Gregor deserved their medals, and their help had enabled me to shoot the lights out as far as my Olympic expectations were concerned, and to surprise a few people along the way – not least the Brits, who maybe rued the day they didn't take me a little more seriously at the start.

I was delighted for my three mates and, like so much about my skeleton career, being in medal contention was only a *happy accident*. The journey had been remarkable enough as it was, a search for the ghost of my father ending up with me becoming an Olympian. However, I don't believe in luck, you have to put yourself in positions to be lucky, and it's also true that the harder you work, the luckier you get.

Coming so close, and the reaction in Ireland, made me determined to secure a future for the sport in Ireland. I approached Pat McDonagh in the Irish Bobsleigh and Luge Association and with the help of the Olympic Council of Ireland, as it was then, established a fund to help half-a-dozen Irish athletes train for skeleton. Of those, Dave Connolly (Turin 2006), Pat Shannon (Vancouver 2010) and Aoife Honey (bobsleigh in 2010) have all become Olympians.

Another one, Brendan Doyle, the former Garda who re-built his life with his skeleton career, narrowly missed out on his dream of making it to Beijing in 2022, but his story is another lesson in hope and perseverance overcoming adversity.

Having been Chef de Mission for the Irish team at the 2006 Winter Olympics in Italy, I was asked by my old mate, Simon Timson, who later became Performance Director at UK Sport, to chair the British Skeleton Association, which has overseen some incredible results with the likes of Amy Williams and Lizzie Yarnold, both plucked from track and field, and winning three Olympic Gold Medals between them.

I'm still part of the high-performance management group for British Skeleton but am now Chair of Ice Hockey UK. I strongly feel that the British example could be replicated in Ireland. As a sport, skeleton presents opportunities to *manufacture* medals.

As the Brits have proven, you can take a sport like skeleton where not an awful lot of nations are at the very top level, and where athletes' talents are transferable, and manufacture medals by creating a winning mentality, with a good talent identification system and high-performance programme. Ireland doesn't have a track, but neither does Britain and they have turned what could be a weakness into a super strength, because they can go around all the tracks in the world, practising, whereas Germany have three tracks and has to focus all their training on those.

There are certain disciplines in sports where talent can be identified and then developed. And I don't see any reason why Ireland can't repeat or even go one better than I did at the Olympics.

You follow the talent and then develop that talent. Ireland has a huge diaspora and there's nothing wrong with taking advantage of that, because there might be someone there who inspires a lot of young Irish kids and opens up opportunities, like my fourth place did for the likes of David, Pat, Aoife, Brendan and the other kids we took out to the Alps for their first runs down a frozen, slippery ice chute.

There's plenty of talent in Ireland. All it takes is a bit of vision, a bit of ambition and a bit of courage. You have to be willing to give it a go.

I gave it a go twenty years ago in Salt Lake City and am still remembered, not for winning, but simply for doing precisely that, giving it a go, and giving it my best.

It's a pretty unlikely story, about a noble Irishman who went to the Swiss Alps to discover more about his dead father, and came within half a second of an Olympic medal.

If I can do it, so can you; there's no such word as *'can't'*!

My Picnic Wish in the Park

Mary Catherine Murray

I have often thought about what it means to make a wish while thinking of someone else's happiness. I have come to believe that it is a powerful force of goodness that supports that person, whether or not the actual wish comes true, and in relation to that, I would like to tell you about my astonishing picnic wish in the park.

It was the summer of 1982. I had recently won a scholarship to study History at Hebrew University in Israel, and was walking with one of my colleagues, Alan, through a park near the beautiful city of Haifa. We passed a huge ancient oak tree with cool, spreading branches and a very wide trunk, where two ladies sat with their backs against the trunk. As we passed, one of them rose quickly and motioned to us to sit down with them. The lady approaching us had a kind face and striking blue eyes. To me, she looked to be about 60 years old. I glanced at the woman who accompanied her and guessed she was perhaps 30. She had the same kind expression, and curling hair, and I concluded that they were mother and daughter. The second lady was holding a baby of about six months.

Both now wanted us to join them under the oak, and Alan was glad to do so as we had been walking in the intense heat all day. I was a little shy and hung back, but then the first lady pointed to a large picnic basket on the grass beside them – it seemed to me that she had prepared it with the intention of sharing. She opened it in the cool of the oak's shade, and removed a large pristine white cloth, spreading it out beside us. She took out homemade pickles, hard-boiled eggs stuffed with mayonnaise and chives, garden tomatoes, roast chicken with fresh lemon and olives, and a semolina cake, flavoured with orange, and a sugared crust. I thought this lady's picnic was lovely, but I was more fascinated with her little granddaughter.

The baby had bright red, curly hair and the same brilliant blue eyes as her grandmother. But she was unusually quiet, and did not move her head in response to all the birds, leaves, and small children fluttering around nearby. The baby's mother spoke English, and when I asked where the family were from, she told me that they had travelled from their home in Nazareth. I continued to be drawn to the baby, as I usually was with all babies, and asked if I could hold her. 'Of course!' was the response, and I gently lifted her from her mother's knee.

The little one was very placid and accepted my lap with contentment. But as I sat with her, I again noted how unusually calm she was. The bright sun entering through the tree branches did not seem to disturb her, and she did not squint at it, or squirm, as my baby sister always had.

I passed my hand slowly in front of her eyes. She did not blink. Her mother confirmed that the baby could not see. 'Her name here is Aether, which means *light of heaven.*'

My friend Alan had other priorities in Haifa rather than darling babies. He had eaten all his semolina cake and was eager to move on to new sights and sounds in the city. I could not account for my feeling of strong connection to the baby, except that my mother had often reminded me of the good fortune I had received in life through my own challenges with childhood illness. She had tapped me on the shoulder at the airport and said, 'Remember to wish everyone there well. Life can be difficult.'

It was time to say good-bye. I could not stay with Aether any longer. I asked her mother if it would be all right if I kissed her goodbye. 'Please do!' she smiled. I kissed the baby and then whispered into her ear my strong, most fervent wish that she would do anything she wanted to do in her life and would be happy. Alan and I walked out of the park and I knew that I would never forget her. I have not been in Israel since that time.

One Saturday morning, in 2012, I went through the main entrance of Debenhams, in Henry Street, and took the escalator to the first floor, where I was hoping to find something for my mother's birthday. Beside the escalator, there was a large table set up with a series of bowls filled with warm water and stacks of clean towels. It was a demonstration stand for a skin scrub and hand cream on sale in the lobby. I rushed past it to get up to the sale.

As I came down the escalator, probably a couple of hours later, and clutching my mother's present, people were departing the store, and venturing out into the summer evening. There was almost noone in the lobby. The dark-haired girl at the demonstration stand motioned for me to come and sit down for a hand treatment. I was shy and hung back, but she had a kind expression.

'I just want to do it', she said. 'You don't have to buy anything, just let me give you a treatment.'

When I heard her accent, I knew immediately she was from Israel. I told her about how I had studied there many years before, and I asked her where she was from, and what she would like to do in life. She told me she came from Haifa and would be returning in a week.

She had studied for a diploma in providing treatments with completely natural cosmetics that would not cause difficulties for those with sensitivities or undergoing cancer treatment. She and her best friend were committed to furthering the wellbeing of anyone who came to the salon they were setting up there.

I remained calm, but I already knew as this lovely girl continued to speak. Her friend was particularly dedicated to this aspect of wellness and beauty care because of her own experiences in life … having vision challenges … finishing her studies…

I asked her quietly about her friend but I really didn't need to. She was from Nazareth, she had bright blue eyes and curly red hair. I already knew her name. The girl at the stand was astounded that I knew her friend and I asked her to please tell Aether she had met an Irish lady who had wished her well all those years ago, and now was so proud that she was doing so much for others in such a committed way in her life. I was so glad to have the chance to know what she had done with her talents and her gift of sensitivity to others.

So, if you are ever in Israel and come across an all-natural beauty salon with two very compassionate therapists, one of whom has bright red hair, definitely go in for a treatment. The therapeutic effects may stay with you for the rest of your life. A full picnic basket is optional.

Our Perfect Pandemic Puppies

Kate Durrant

It's a humbling thing to sit with a dog while she labours; doing her best, her big eyes filled with bewilderment, trusting you all the way. Whilst you, with no words to console her, can't help but feel you've let her down as she pushes through pain that she has no way of understanding.

Jennifer, founder of the charity 'Dogs for Disabled', has been with Jasmine in the whelping box for hours now cajoling and encouraging her to release her pups. I have no doubt that if she could, she would have them for her.

We've been fostering dogs for this wonderful charity for six years now. Ivy was the first to steal our hearts. A stunningly gorgeous retriever with a soul as golden as her coat, and the start of a most wonderful journey of fun and fur, wet walks and waggy tails, and hellos and goodbyes. Ivy was born, and spent her first important eight weeks, in the Dochas Centre at Mountjoy Prison through a unique partnership between the prison and the charity, before coming to live with us to be socialised.

And socialise us she did as she christened our carpets, chewed our slippers, and knocked down the fences surrounding our garden, and our hearts, before leaving eighteen months later to train to become the partner and best friend to Noah, a very special small boy who needed her far more than we did.

With Ivy gone, a steady stream of weekend and holiday visitors left their muddy paw prints on our couches, and in our hearts, as they snuffled their way in and out of our home shedding fur and love in equal measure in their wake.

Some slept on the cushions that litter our floor like stepping stones, others took their rightful place with us on the couch, and, as assistants to the assistance dogs, we became excellent walkers, professional hooverers, and bakers of the most wonderful peanut-butter cookies.

Temporary guests aside, our permanent four-legged family also continued to grow. Handsome Hugo, a majestic black Labrador who takes his job as a therapy dog in the local hospital very seriously, was followed by Fleur, who had given her life to the service of others and who, when she retired, slipped into our lives like she had been there forever. And last, but certainly not least, came Jasmine, placed with us five years earlier as an eight-week-old puppy, and part of the Dogs for Disabled ethical breeding programme.

This little family of four legs (and two) sat quietly together in the wee small hours of the morning as Jasmine laboured, my beautiful dog never breaking eye contact with me for one minute as her body convulsed with contractions, and Hugo and Fleur dozed at my feet with one eye open, not moving an inch. It got to 4.00 a.m., and worry had set in with the realisation that the first pup was stuck, putting not only his own little life at risk, but also the lives of the litter to follow and, most importantly, his mother.

A tense dash across the city followed, and the vet, roused from sleep, used his skill to release the first little miracle, allowing Jasmine to complete her labour, gifting us six beautiful healthy future assistance dogs that will go on to change the lives of small children with big dreams to walk.

KATE DURRANT

As their little eyes slowly opened so too did ours and, through them, we saw the unfolding beauty of the unnaturally quiet pandemic world they were born into one of the most turbulent times in our history.

As the nation clapped for nurses we clapped for our small guests when they learnt to pee outside and, with no interest in the nightly figures on the news, and unable to move more than two hundred metres, never mind two kilometres, we embraced every magical moment of lockdown as they turned our home into a wonderful adventure course: crawling under our couches, climbing up our curtains and burrowing deep into our hearts.

As case numbers fell and restrictions lifted, and life returned to pre-Covid busyness, the day came when our ten-week-old balls of fluff left us to start out on their own very special journey. With no vaccine to protect us against the pain of them leaving, and their abandoned water bowls looking up at us, we cried as we said goodbye to these six precious bundles of four-legged joy who, at the end of a long, cold winter night, snuffled their way into that place deep in our core that had been home to our small children, now taller and not needing to be held there anymore.

As I write this I catch sight of the chewed leg of a much loved squeaky chicken peeking out from under the couch, and I think of a time in years to come when my grandchildren will ask me, 'What did you do during lockdown Granny?' and I can sit them down and tell them the story of Neville, Nancy, Nollaig, Niall, Noddy, and Professor Neil Green, our perfect, pandemic, puppies.

Emma

Damien Ballout

Ninety-four percent of those who experience what my wife went through are, sadly, no longer with us. So, every morning when I look at the smile on Emma's face, I realise that I am one of the lucky ones, and her survival is due, in part, to the Covid-19 pandemic that was sweeping the world and killing thousands.

Just one month into lockdown, on 30 April 2020, I was working from home, on a business call, when I heard a scream bellowing up the stairs. Emma was on maternity leave and I was accustomed to various shouts and screams from Henry, our happy two-year-old, and George, our six-month-old baby, but this was different – I'd never heard one like it before, and it's one I will never forget. My mum, Ann-Marie, who lives next door, had joined us for lunch and it was she who was shouting. 'Damien, Emma has fallen!' The loudness and urgency in the call, the screams of a baby in pain, and the cries of a scared toddler told me something was seriously wrong!

In the kitchen, Emma was lying on the floor, Henry, a few feet away, looked terrified, and my mum was holding George. 'Emma fell on top of George, I had to get her off him – quick Damien!' I could see Emma was lifeless on the floor and started to check for signs of life: pulse, clear airways, was she breathing? Mum called for an ambulance and I put Emma in the recovery position, and then realised it wasn't the correct thing to be doing.

I've never had any first aid or CPR training but would have read and seen enough material on it to have some sort of idea of what to do. I started CPR and had a serious case of imposter syndrome, 'Who am I trying to kid – I don't know what I'm doing'. But I did know I needed to keep on going until help arrived, it was up to me to keep doing something, anything, to keep Emma with us. Henry was swinging on my neck during the compressions, joining in, thinking it was a game.

After what felt like forever: I saw Fiona come running through the kitchen door from the garden wearing full PPE – she is a family friend who was at our wedding four years previously. It felt like everything went in slow motion when Fiona arrived, my brain did not process what was happening, why was Fiona running in my kitchen? Why was she wearing full PPE, almost unrecognisable? Should I offer her a cup of tea?

The answer was soon obvious: Fiona was the first paramedic on the scene and assertively told me to continue the compressions while she got the defibrillator ready and then shocked Emma. Was this really happening? You only see this stuff on TV. Two more paramedics arrived, administering two more shocks to Emma before getting a heart rhythm. Another three paramedics arrived to attend to Baby George. At this point I still didn't know what had happened.

Emma went off in one ambulance to Connolly Hospital, I was in another ambulance with George heading for Temple Street and my mum stayed behind to mind Henry. In the ambulance I called Emma's mum, Mary, and told her Emma had had a fall and was being taken to hospital and I needed her to come to Temple Street. I could not bring myself to tell Mary the severity of what had just happened. I had to call her sister, Lynne, to tell her.

When Mary arrived at Temple Street, the doctor came off the phone and said someone needed to be with Emma now. I didn't know what to do. I couldn't leave my baby here, he needed me or his mum. Mary stayed with George, and Emma's dad, Pat, drove me to Connolly. It was a quiet journey! In the hospital they took me to the relatives' room. Again, this was something I'd only seen on TV before, and I feared the worst. I was alone in the room, trying to go over the madness of the past couple of hours when Emma's sister, Lynne, and brother, John, arrived. I didn't have any answers, I couldn't explain what had happened. The doctors told us that Emma had suffered a cardiac arrest and was very ill. It was hard to grasp, we were having lunch together a few hours ago, laughing, joking, everything was normal. To my mind, somebody with no underlying health conditions doesn't just have a cardiac arrest only a few weeks past their thirty-eighth birthday!

Emma was transferred to the Mater Hospital and placed in the intensive care unit. The doctors allowed me a few minutes with her before she went in. It felt like I was supposed to say goodbye, but I couldn't – I whispered, 'Please come home Emma, I can't do this without you, me and the boys need you.' I got home late that evening and George was back after being checked over. The house was full but silent. Emma's family, her son Jack, my family, even Fiona the paramedic, called over, all of us trying to understand and make sense of what had happened. I lay awake all night in floods of tears, how was I going to tell the boys their mummy wasn't coming home? Could I have done something differently? How was I going to feed George, he had always refused bottles and was exclusively breastfed. I tried feeding him, no joy. He would fight so hard refusing to take the bottle that he would be exhausted and sleep without feeding.

Next morning, I tried keeping it together for the boys, trying to keep some sort of normality, but I found myself in floods of tears, crying on my mum's shoulder saying, 'I need to be positive, I need to think positively but I can't do it, I don't think she is coming back.' Emma spent two nights in ICU; I was briefly allowed to see her from behind closed doors, dressed in full PPE. I regularly spoke with the doctors, who said she was comfortable and reiterated the seriousness of what had happened. She just looked like she was having a sleep. I took solace from seeing her and it ignited some positivity in me, I felt uplifted and hopeful.

The following day I got a call to say Emma's eyes had opened, and they were following the nurse's movements around the room. A sense of relief: the first real bit of news, and it was positive. I had been told that due to the seriousness of the cardiac arrest and the length of time before Emma's heart was restarted, it was highly likely that Emma may have lost some of the function of her brain. When I arrived at the hospital, the nurse said Emma was awake, but she wasn't talking. When I looked in her eyes she followed me round the room and I knew that my Emma was still here. She took off her oxygen mask and said how sorry she was. I had to leave when she was taken up to the Cardiac Care unit for the next stage of her recovery, but in my mind Emma was safe and well, the boys still had their mummy.

George was still not feeding so I had to bring him back into Temple Street. Deep down I knew it was the right thing to do but I felt like I was failing him, not being able to give him something his mum had done effortlessly and seamlessly. Once again I found myself in tears on the way to the hospital. George was admitted to Temple Street, and I was put at ease by the warm, caring team at the hospital. Emma's mum was going to stay with George.

I went to visit Emma in CCU, and she was incredibly agitated, confused, not knowing where she was, why she was in there, and why they had taken her young baby from her. This continued for hours with her removing all the wires and trying to get up and leave the hospital. It was mentally and physically exhausting but she finally fell asleep, and the doctors told me that this was normal after being sedated. That night Emma was calling me, her mum, and whoever else, on her phone, asking them to pick her up and help her escape from the prison she was being kept in.

The next day I went to Temple Street to visit George and then onto Emma for another round of trying to comfort her and persuade her to stay, with her not being able to process what had happened, or believe it.

Again, after a full day of Emma trying to escape, with hospital staff and myself reassuring her, trying to reason with her, and after her calling the police saying she had been kidnapped and being held hostage in the Mater in Cork, she finally went to sleep in my arms.

I went back across the road to Temple Street where I got a cuddle from George and now he went to sleep in my arms; he was finally starting to feed but was being kept in until he was fully established. At last I was able to go home to Henry, who was with my mum. In her garden, my two-year-old son asked me, 'Daddy, when are Mummy and Georgie coming home?' I found myself in tears again, desperately trying to hold them back. I finally put Henry to sleep that night, he had hardly gone a day in his life without seeing his mummy and, since his recent arrival, his little brother, and now they had both gone.

George was home the next day, fully established on the bottle and feeding well, thanks to a determined Nana Mary and the fantastic team in Temple Street. Things were going in the right direction; Emma was being a bit more reasonable and starting to understand what was happening. The escape plan continued though as she worked her way through her phone book trying to get someone to help her break out. I spent every day at the hospital with Emma, all the time noticing big improvements. She was going to have an ICD inserted, which would help her heart if it stopped again.

After thirteen nights in hospital we got the news that Emma was coming home. She would finally get to see her family, loved ones and most importantly her boys: Henry, George, and Jack. She had done it; she had defied the odds. Only six percent of those who suffer a cardiac arrest at home survive; my best friend was one of those, and she was coming home.

The farewell at the CCU was an emotional one, the staff there had provided exemplary care for Emma, and I felt part of the team. One of the nurses told Emma I had been there day and night, and words that stuck with her when we were trying to stop her from escaping was a comment I had made: 'We are all in this together Emma, we are with you.' The short drive home from the Mater was very peaceful, Emma was taking in all the sights and saying how clean the air was, how green the trees were and how blue the skies were. We were both super excited and I was super proud to be driving her back home to the boys and her family.

The truth is that we were all in it together, the nurses, the doctors, consultants, paramedics, ambulance service, the control room, my mum on hand to alert me and call for an ambulance, my attempt at CPR, which was only possible because I was working from home due to the pandemic. That day we all clicked as a team, everyone stepped up and we won, and I will forever be grateful to everyone who contributed. There are too many people to thank individually, but I do want to mention our five-year-old nephew, Oscar, who wrote a very touching note to his teacher.

The days and weeks that followed in getting Emma back on her feet and home to us was down to top-class healthcare from the medical professionals of the ambulance service, Connolly Hospital, and the Mater ICU and CCU. The real star of the story though is you, Emma; you nearly left us on that day in April, but you never gave up, you fought incredibly hard to be one of the six percent and to make a speedy recovery. You came home to your baby, George, who was now knocking back bottles of milk and happy as ever, to our little bundle of joy Henry, who might now hold the record for the youngest person to successfully administer CPR, and to a loving husband who went on an unforgettable and emotional journey.

> Dear Ms Megannety
> My auntie is very sick.
> But my uncle Saved
> her Live by doing C.P.R
> She is getting better
> your Student Oscar

DARWIN

Robert Alderson

The summer of 2014 proved to be a wholly exciting one for me, allowing me to combine two of my great passions. The first, as a singing teacher, is a passion for finding raw singing talent and nurturing it. The second is travel, with numerous visits to Egypt and India under my belt.

During that summer I was invited to give vocal masterclasses in New Delhi for the Neemrana Foundation, a non-profit organisation promoting Western classical music in India, and it was during the last week of my visit that I first met a young man named Darwin Prakash. He had come along with some of his friends to watch, rather than participate in, the classes, at the end of which the little group gathered outside, singing and having a good time, when I heard this very exciting, albeit very raw, baritone *sound.* I went outside, saw it was Darwin, and asked him why he didn't sing in class. He told me that he would never have thought he was good enough to be included.

I disagreed wholeheartedly with his assessment and saw huge potential in his voice, so for the rest of my visit I gave him a one-hour lesson at seven o'clock every morning. His voice came on in leaps and bounds. It was clear that he was highly intelligent and well educated, and I was delighted with his innate musicality and, importantly, his work ethic. Before leaving India, I asked a great friend, and fellow singing teacher, to give him lessons and to introduce him to the Italian and German languages. At that time, Darwin was twenty-one years old, had just finished a degree in Geology, and was unemployed.

The young man had made a big impression on me and on my return to England, I decided to contact his parents seeking their permission to bring him to Manchester. My plan was to give him intense lessons before presenting him to the Royal Academy of Music in London where he would audition for the postgraduate vocal performance programme. A few months later, in December 2014, a young, excited, and very cold, Darwin Leonard Prakash arrived in Manchester to follow what was now his dream – to become an opera singer.

Everything had been arranged. He was to live in my home as part of our family. Friends took him shopping to provide him with winter clothing. A great friend of my family, with a passion for opera, gave him a small monthly allowance so that he would have money in his pocket.

It was no easy task, but throughout that winter Darwin worked extremely hard, learning how to read music and the vocal repertoire. We did vocal exercises every morning, theory classes every afternoon, and learned a lot of the repertoire he would need for entry to music college.

In February 2015, just three months after he had left India, I arranged for him to apply for the Glyndebourne Opera education training course for outstanding young vocal talents. His audition was successful and he took part in the course that summer.

Amazingly, Darwin was also successful in getting a full scholarship to study at the Royal Academy of Music in London where he completed his MA in vocal performance in 2017. His work ethic, that was obvious during his initial lessons in India, was always to the fore as he went on, two years later, to achieve an Advanced Diploma in Opera from the Royal Academy of Music. During his four years of study in London, he performed a number of operatic roles and each year was awarded a scholarship, prize or commendation. It was also here, at the academy, that he met the young lady who would later become his wife.

Subsequent to college, he became a member of the International Opera Studio at Stationer in Hannover, Germany, where he sung many baritone roles to great acclaim. In the summer of 2022 he was appointed a full salaried principal singer at the Hannover State Opera where he now sings principal baritone roles. An amazing achievement for anyone, but especially for a young man who only took his first singing lesson a mere eight years previously.

While his career as an opera singer continues to flourish, he has become a fully integrated member of my family. His parents have come from India to visit him at my home and he joins us there whenever he has time off from the opera house. In September 2022 we were honoured to host his family and friends from India for a pre-wedding celebration, and to be guests at the ceremony in Staffordshire.

A chance encounter in a land far away has changed the life of one young Indian man, and enriched the lives of all of us in Europe and beyond who have met him, or heard him, in the ensuing years.

THE FOX AT THE PLAZA

Bernadette O'Sullivan

We left Kerry under the awning of a sly November sky, with clouds lying low and grey to perfectly match my mood, pathetic fallacy at its best. It was the eve of my young son's annual oncology review, a date in the calendar to be approached in equal measure of celebration and trepidation. The former because another year cancer-free had been reached and the latter because life had taught me that circumstance can change in the blink of an eye. Six years prior we had walked into Temple Street hospital for a diagnostic procedure that was simple and left with a diagnosis that was anything but.

On this particular evening, however, we drove familiar roads at ease, our companiable silence interspersed with chats about school and the latest conquests, or not, of Manchester United, whom my son had met the previous year through Make-A-Wish Ireland. It wasn't just a wish come true, but rather a dream come true, for my boy who's hero was, and still is, David de Gea. About three hours into the journey we stopped at a well-known plaza frequented by weary travellers. Despite the month of the year and the hour of the day, the car park was particularly busy and we had to circle twice to find a parking spot relatively close to the entrance. On the second circuit we were amazed to see a lone fox sitting on a small grassy area near where we intended to park. I slowed the car to a halt and viewed this beautiful creature as he regally viewed us in turn. Our reverie was broken only by the chatter of exiting customers from the plaza and he scampered into the nearby bushes, quickly disappearing from our sight.

Thirty minutes later we exited, having completed our ablutions and refuelled car and passengers alike only to see the fox again sitting nearby like a lonely sentry. I know that my own maternal instincts were on high alert that night due to what faced us the following day, but the fox did portray a particularly lonely figure, so I knew that I couldn't drive on and leave him hungry. We entered the plaza for a second time, approached the counter of Supermacs and perused the menu. I probably should apologise to Wildlife Ireland at this point but I had never faced such a situation before, so I wasn't sure what the best course of action was for a hungry-looking fox.

We have all heard the story of the fox in the proverbial henhouse so I figured that a chicken burger was probably the best choice. On placing my order, the girl behind the counter asked if I would like lettuce, onions and mayo with the burger but I politely declined thinking that the fox may not thank me for a bout of indigestion. We paid and walked outside to the area where we had last seen him. I unwrapped the burger, placed it on the ground, and then waited in the car to see our Good Samaritan act unfold. Well, unfold it soon did as the fox reappeared. Before he got to the burger a big black cat burst from the undergrowth, and like a nocturnal ninja swiped at the bun, grabbed the burger and made off with his juicy spoil between his jaws, all the while being watched by me, my open-mouthed son and a stunned fox.

I wasn't sure whether the situation was comedic or tragic but, either way, I knew I didn't have time to place a repeat order, so I quietly apologised to the fox, urged him to enjoy his meal of carbohydrate, and we continued on our journey to Dublin. We have travelled that road, and visited the same establishment many times since, but despite always being on the look, out we have never since caught sight of the fox.

I can only hope that he is alive and well and that life has been good to him, just as it has been to my young son who, I am blessed to say, as I write this, is just a month away from his thirteenth birthday.

THE CHOIR

Johanne Powell

It started at a lunch. A group from Family Carers Ireland were lunching with representatives of Tyrone Productions when the discussion turned to the fabulous success of the 'homeless' choir, properly called the 'High Hopes Choir'. Someone said, 'Why not start a choir of carers?' And someone else suggested asking David Brophy (one of Ireland's most distinguished conductors) to take it on. Tyrone Productions would create a documentary about the project.

The concept was to show carers both in and out of their caring roles, having some fun far away from their daily struggle. It could provide some insight into carers' lives, which are hidden from most people. It would be an uplifting and fun programme for the audience and provide participants a chance to meet and mix with other carers. Many carers feel guilty about taking time out from their caring roles, and maybe something very different like this might make it easier for them.

Wexford would be the birthplace, an area well known for its musical inhabitants. The word went out to carers all over the Southeast and people joined from Kilkenny, Carlow, Wicklow and even Dublin. I was 'volunteered' by so-called friends to join, even though I don't have a note in my body!

On a wet January day, we met in Castlebridge, outside Wexford, for interviews to assess our suitability and, to my utter surprise, I was accepted. No doubt it helped that our singing voices were not examined, just our general friendliness and criteria fulfilment, i.e. we were family carers or ex-carers for *somebody*! Plenty of tea, coffee and biscuits, with tons of chats, and jokes, became a recurring theme over the next few months.

We (well, Tyrone Productions, but 'we' sounds better) decided to have fortnightly rehearsals in Castlebridge, stepping up to weekly as we got closer to important performances. We weren't sure what the final event would be, but we knew there would be one, and we were nervous. At least I was: an impostor without a voice!

Two weeks later we gathered in the hall with pictures on the walls from long-gone days, seated on the usual hard 'hall' chairs, when the door sprang open and in bounced the mad, enthusiastic, wonderful conductor, David Brophy. What I remember best of that first day was when he was trying to teach us to tap our feet. To show us better, he jumped up on the windowsill so we could properly see his excellent foot tapping! He talked and played and chatted and bounced, and in between we even sang a bit (though some of us mimed, and some of us sang quietly to ourselves.) It was great fun and we left that day full of bounce, vim and vigour.

Being an internationally known conductor, David Brophy also had other commitments, so to help shape us into suitable choristers, we were introduced to the universally agreed *wonderful* conductor that is Eithne Corrigan. That poor woman: she played and cajoled and bullied and coaxed us, and she taught us all new things. Who knew that professional singers like us(!) needed exercises to loosen up our voices? Well, personally I kept my voice under rather tight control, but you get the idea. She taught us what a conductor's hand signal means and how to keep in tune (or try). A concert is a performance, so we learnt to move with the music, put emotion in our singing and not stand glued to the spot with faces like dead fish. We discovered that some of us did not have great listening skills, and that it can be difficult to shut up while instruction is being given.

We also found that some of us had great voices and some of the voices had names, like contralto and bass and tenor and mezzo-soprano! It all sounded wonderful, even for those amongst us who knew we had none of those, but voices more readily compared to rooks and crows.

As time went on, we made new friends, we discovered common cause in our caring roles and our battles with the HSE, the Department of Health, Department of Education, politicians, ourselves, the people we cared for and loved ... in short, our lives of never-ending battles. We had our very first concert in Galway during the FCI carers' respite weekend. It was wonderful to perform in front of a room full of other carers, and the love flowing both ways was palpable. We weren't terribly good, but we were very enthusiastic.

Tyrone Productions visited several of our choir members to see and document the daily struggle and love that took place in our homes. Evan Johnston's mother, a young widow whose two sons had autism, allowed the cameras in for a night, and it was an eyeopener. For me the high point of that visit was when Evan, who is severely autistic and is generally non-verbal, managed to say 'I love you' to his mother.

In Clonard they visited Betty and Phil and their son Jason, and there was not a dry eye in the place when Phil sang 'My Forever Friend' to his son. Phil and Betty told me later that after the programme was aired that they were recognised on a Sunday drive at an ice-cream van, but they got no free ice cream! Shame. There were also other home visits, involving that most cruel of diseases, dementia. It showed in a sensitive, real way, the life some of us live.

Over the weeks we got to know each other, learning what other people had to cope with. Some looked after parents, others – children or adult sons and daughters, others again – spouses. Some had lost their loved ones, others still had them. We cried and we laughed, and most of all, we sang!

JOHANNE POWELL

Slowly, very slowly, we started to feel like a choir, and early in June had our second official outing, singing on the steps of Johnstown Castle in front of our friends and relatives. We had a glorious day, the sun shone and so did we in our bright summer clothes. We had a picnic in the grounds and listened to the screeches of the peacocks. I think for most of us, that day was one of the real highlights of our experiences, and when Fiona's little son tried to crawl up to her as she was standing on the steps singing, it was magical.

Planning was now going ahead for what would be the finale of the programme, and David Brophy invited Cork-based singer-songwriter John Spillane to talk to us and write a song based on our own words and stories. So, 'Real Heroes Go Unsung' was born. It is extra special to all of us in the choir since it is *our* song.

The finale would be a concert in Wexford's National Opera House on Midsummer night. It would launch an awareness campaign by Family Carers Ireland called 'Shine a Light', on the longest day of the year, to remind people about the long nights, and days, carers spend working with, and for, the people we love, with little or no, or at best, woefully inadequate, support.

Then a second *big* surprise, with extra special visitors! First was Aslan, confirming that they would be taking part in our final concert! Well, there were whoops of joy and much excitement, and photos – what we would have done without smartphones I don't know! Unfortunately, this part of the concert had to be cancelled, but we certainly enjoyed it while it lasted.

Davy Fitzgerald, the then manager of the Wexford hurling team, was next, talking to us about motivation and commitment and such things, and singing 'The Purple and Gold'. To be honest, most Wexford choristers were keen on finding out Davy's view on the coming season, and having their photos taken with him rather than anything else. I did hear mutterings from the Kilkenny crowd, but we're used to 'the Cats' whinging in Wexford, so we ignored it!

Final rehearsals were really taking off now. We had to learn the lyrics, how to enter and leave the stage, where to stand, even how to sit down to avoid the chair skidding away from us! Soloists were picked (nobody will be surprised to hear I was not even an also-ran in that selection!). Outfits had to be organised with a black and purple colour scheme. Have you any idea how difficult it is to find something purple in Wexford in June? Men had it easy, they only needed a tie! We also got a name; we were now officially the 'Real Heroes Choir'.

The day finally arrived. We were so excited. We rocked up in the morning all agog, ready for the adventure. Even getting to the stage was an adventure. Luckily for the performance we didn't have to climb up onto the stage from the auditorium. God, those steps were high!

We had a couple of run-throughs, got star struck when Gavin James entered to set up his kit, walked on and off the stage several times to get it right, got starstruck again when Eleanor McEvoy came in to look us over and ask us to sing along with her for her performance of 'A Woman's Heart' on the night.

We had a quick lunch at the top of the Opera House and admired the wonderful view over the harbour. More training – who knew all the preparation needed for these things? We stood and sat, we sang and soloed, soloed and sang again, we moved up and down to make sure nobody was being overshadowed by the taller choristers. Music and microphones were tested and tested again, spots were marked on stage for soloists to stand. All told, it was great fun.

But all fun comes to an end, and it was time to get all dressed up for the performance of our life. A couple of us got lost in the warren of rooms behind the stage. Luckily the sound of our fellow choristers whispering reached farther than you would think, and we were able to catch up and sneak into our designated places in the long conga-line waiting to enter the stage. We could hear the rustle and chat of the audience in the auditorium. The curtains swung open, David Brophy gave a short introduction, and we were on! We filed in, miraculously managing to not fall off the stage or trip over each other.

We sang the John Spillane song, 'Real Heroes Go Unsung' with John, Gavin James sang, we sang again, Eleanor McEvoy sang and we sang along with her! On the screen behind us photos of the people we care for were being projected in a steady stream. The audience clapped and cheered and laughed and cried with us and a wonderful evening was had by us all. When the concert finished, to rapturous applause and standing ovations, some of the audience were heard saying: 'My God, they sounded professional'.

A party went on long and hard in a certain pub not far from the Opera House, and more quiet celebrations took place in hotels and bars and homes across town. It was a wonderful night, and seemed a fitting end to the project. Not that the choir was finishing, we were continuing, but Tyrone Productions would be moving on with editing and production and new projects.

Every year Family Carers Ireland holds a celebration called 'Carer of the Year'. The highlight is a lunch in Dublin's five-star Westin Hotel. Somebody had the absolutely brilliant idea to get the Real Heroes Choir to sing at that event.

We were more than willing and excited at the thought of performing in front of our peers. David was away, but Eithne was more than capable of sorting us out with a couple of extra rehearsals where she smartened us up and drilled us hard. The purple and black was dug out again and a bus from Wexford was arranged. Others arrived in trains and cars or whatever contraptions they could lay their hands on.

The Westin is a stunning hotel in the centre of Dublin. It was originally built as the headquarters of the Provincial Bank, one of the three main banks in Ireland, and my, does it look like it – marble and crystal, liveried staff, even a doorman, fully kitted out, to let you in and out (far from the sort of thing we were reared on).

The hotel laid on a wonderful spread for carers from across the country, and we were brought onto the stage to perform several songs from our rapidly expanding repertoire. To see the carers decked out in their finery amongst the silver and crystal, porcelain and marble, to be able to share with them our joy of music, it was a truly wonderful experience.

So, we were now waiting for the release of the wonderful documentary, which had been expanded into two episodes because we were such wonderful subjects. Unforeseen events meant the release was postponed and postponed again, until eventually being released after the Covid-19 pandemic hit.

Originally we planned to get to together, crack open the champagne and celebrate, but Covid put paid to that. Instead we met online, with champagne and tea and wine and drinks and chocolates and whatever celebratory fancies we wanted! It was such an emotional experience, to see us all a full year earlier, to see all the strangers who are now firm friends, to remember people since passed on, to hear ourselves for the first time (as you can't really hear when you are singing yourself). The programme was a hit, and went on to win first prize in RTS Ireland Television Awards for best factual series.

Unfortunately, Covid-19 stopped us all in our tracks, including the choir. I believe there are plans to bring it together again, but as the non-singing, non-dancing chorister, I think I will bow out graciously here.

The choir had brought us together allowing us to share our grief and our joy, our highs and our lows, our tears and our laughter, and to build new and lasting friendships.

It was a truly wonderful experience.

KATHLEEN

Stephen Breen

On 23 May 2022, I was interviewed by the RTÉ team behind the *Case I Can't Forget* programme. The documentary – featuring contributions from witnesses and journalists, along with no longer serving and retired members of An Garda Síochána – concentrates on some of Ireland's most high-profile criminal cases.

To date, some of the previous hour-long episodes have focused on the murder of Rachel Callaly by her husband Joe O'Reilly and Dublin's heroin epidemic in the 1980s. However, this time around, my contribution to the programme would be in relation to the murders of ten-year-old Eoghan Chada and his five-year-old brother Ruairi, by their father, Sanjeev, on 29 July 2013.

Like the many terrible tragedies that have occurred over the course of my career, I remember where I was when news of the double murders broke on a warm summer day nine years earlier. As the awful news unfolded, I was sent to Rosbeg in Co Mayo where the bodies of the two brothers had been recovered from the boot of their father's car.

Shortly after arriving at the scene, I was welcomed into the home of one of the men who made the shocking discovery of the brothers' lifeless bodies after their father had crashed his car into a wall.

A few days later, on 2 August 2013, the nation was united in grief as the boys' heartbroken mother, Kathleen, laid her only children to rest. And, just as I can remember where I was when news of the terrible deaths broke, I also remember the first time I met Eoghan and Ruairi's remarkable mother.

It was a year after the killings when Kathleen agreed to speak to me about her ongoing trauma but also on her plans to help families who had lost loved ones through murder. Within minutes of meeting her at Dublin's Gresham Hotel, I could see how much she had dearly loved her children. She was now their voice.

Despite suffering a loss that not too many of us can possibly imagine, Kathleen spoke openly about her children and the joys they brought to her life. I was struck not only by the bravery she had shown in speaking about her children, but also about her commitment to helping others. Following the interview, I reflected on a woman who possessed great courage, resilience, determination, humility and kindness.

Some people who have lost loved ones in violent circumstances chose not to share their stories and that is their right. On this occasion, however, Kathleen made the decision to speak to me so she could pay tribute to two boys who had touched so many lives in such a short space of time.

Since that first interview, I have met Kathleen many times. And on each and every occasion, her determination and resilience have shone through just as it did at that first meeting in 2014.

In the years after our first meeting, the focus of our articles was on her ongoing healing and grieving process. But from 2018 onwards, many of our articles focused on Kathleen's attempts to amend Ireland's Parole Bill. At that time, anyone convicted of murder in the State was entitled to apply for parole after seven years. The ruling meant that, in 2021, the man who had claimed the lives of Kathleen's two children could apply for early parole.

However, Kathleen once again showed her determination and resilience to make the Department of Justice take notice when she, along with other grieving families, helped form the Sentencing and Victims' Equality Group (SAVE).

Thanks largely to the group's ongoing pressure on the government, the 2019 Parole Act was later passed. The Act, which meant that life-sentence prisoners could only apply for parole after serving twelve years in prison, would also see the formation of a new parole board, placing victims and their families at the heart of its agenda.

Following the announcement of the new bill, I thought of how proud Kathleen's children would be of their mother. A mother who took on the system – and won.

In 2020, Kathleen also wrote a personal piece for the *Irish Sun* outlining her ongoing efforts to secure change. For her, it was about providing a voice for her two sons and the families of other victims. Without question, it's one of the most powerful articles I have ever read from a grieving mother. In the article, she said:

'I was thrust into a world that I knew nothing about and one I had no control in. I felt as if the judicial system did not really care about me. It was all consumed by Sanjeev. I will continue to fight. I do it for the sake of my sons. I do it for my sake to keep Sanj off the streets and I do it for the sake of all those who will face the same issues and pain that I and so many others face on a weekly basis.'

Kathleen is just one of many grieving parents and siblings who, over the years, have been thrust into the spotlight through no fault of their own.

Alongside her are also some of the bravest women I have ever met through the course of my work, women whose primary concern was to secure justice for their loved ones.

It's impossible to mention them all but people like Bridie Collins, whose sister Sandra has been missing for almost 22 years; Jean O'Connor, who passed away before seeing justice for her son Eoin;

Christine Campbell, whose son Anthony was shot dead simply because he witnessed a gangland murder; and Anne del Cassian, who ensured that two men were convicted of her sister Irene's murder before she passed away, have all shown remarkable courage and strength over the years.

In a fair world, I should never have had to meet people like Kathleen Chada, Bridie Collins, Jean O'Connor, Christine Campbell or Anne del Cassian, but it was through the course of my work that our paths crossed.

For people like Kathleen and many others, I will never forget the strength and determination that they have shown in the midst of such unimaginable horror.

THE SHELL HOUSE

Des Kiely

Cliff Cottage is appropriately named, standing, as it does, on the cliff overlooking Cullenstown Strand with views across Ballyteigue Bay to Kilmore Quay to the east and Hook Head to the west, with the Saltee and Keeragh islands in between. It was in this idyllic spot that Cathy Ffrench, the youngest of five children, spent her childhood years during the 1960s, with her parents, Kevin and Kathy.

Kevin had served in the Royal Navy during the Second World War, signing up when he was just eighteen and joining *HMS Caradoc*, which was deployed in the North Atlantic. By the time he left the service in 1942 he had been awarded three medals.

The cottage dates from around 1700 and still boasts a pitch pine roof that came from shipwrecks which were all too common on the south coast of County Wexford. It had been in Kevin's family for generations and it is where his mother was born, but it had fallen into disrepair. Following their marriage in 1945, Kevin and Kathy spent eleven years living in Bannow, near to Kathy's family, before eventually moving to Cullenstown, with Kevin restoring the cottage himself.

On an adjoining field, in soil enriched with seaweed from the beach, he grew vegetables and kept a few cattle and hens. Added to this, he had a small fishing boat and would sell mackerel, or whatever his catch was that day, from the house.

Cathy, in the meantime, had spent many hours on the beach, collecting shells, bringing them home, and leaving her parents in a quandary – what to do with the huge collection that was cluttering the house. Cathy was adamant that they could not be thrown away. Eventually, Kevin decided to use some of them to decorate an old flowerpot. Pleased with his work, he then added some of them to the tops of the piers at the gate, and then the front wall of the house. And so began thirty years of painstaking work, covering the entire house with seashells; his goal was to leave behind a work of art, a legacy that would survive long after his death.

It was a huge undertaking and he would have to add to Cathy's collection to complete it. The majority of them came from the beach below the cottage, but he also collected razor shells from Rosslare Strand, scallop and mussel shells from the fishermen in Kilmore Quay, and oyster and cockle shells from Bannow Bay. He sorted the shells to find exact matches and meticulously measured each one, using his own handmade seven-inch ruler that had the measurements from right to left.

Sand and cement were used to apply the shells, and when he had finished covering the entire front of the cottage, he moved on to the yard and covered all the out-buildings. The cottage is now stunningly decorated with over 50,000 seashells and amongst the patterns he crafted are beautiful interpretations of Tuskar Light-house, various ships, ships' wheels and sea birds. He also incorporated an old lifebuoy and a porthole from a shipwreck in the designs.

Throughout the winter months, Kevin would work out his designs and then carefully select the correct shells, ready to apply them outside when spring arrived. As a nod to his time in the navy, also found within his artwork is the motto of the Royal Marines: *Per Mare Per Terram* (By Sea, By Land). His last work, on the gable end of the cottage, depicts a large dolphin.

The oat straw thatch on the roof needed replacing every ten years or so, and Kevin learned how to maintain it himself. In 1976 it won Bord Fáilte's *Best Thatched Homestead* award. In October 2017, hurricane Ophelia, the worst storm to affect Ireland in 50 years, tore across Bally-teigue Bay from the North Atlantic and ripped away a large portion of the thatch and some of the shell decorations in the courtyard. The house is one of Ireland's most unique landmarks, photographed by thousands of visitors every year, and being a listed building, a partial grant to entirely re-thatch the cottage in oat straw was approved in 2019.

When Kevin passed away in 2003, at the age of eighty-one, his family erected a plaque on the front of the cottage: '*Dedicated to the memory of Kevin L. Ffrench who designed and crafted the artistic shellwork on this cottage.*'

That the house continues to be photographed by visitors to Cullens-town, who are in awe of his craftsmanship, and that photographs of his great artistic work continue to be shared on social media around the world, are testament to the fact that he achieved his goal to leave behind a legacy that would survive long after his death.

Putting the Word Out

Tom Fathom

My father and I laughed as we struggled to push the heavy cartload of grain up the hill. It was a beautiful autumn day in 1953 and the air was rich with the smell of freshly ploughed fields. Suddenly, without warning, the life left my father's body and he collapsed on the side of the road. He was only 54, I was twelve.

While struggling with the sudden grief and shock, my mother and I also had the fear of not knowing how we would survive without our provider. Because we had fifteen acres of land, we were considered too wealthy for my mother to receive the widow's pension. At the wake and the funeral, friends and neighbours queued up to offer their friendship and support and assured us that they would be there for us if we needed anything. Many were true to their word. Sadly, however, some were not. Indeed, some cruelly capitalised on our devastating predicament.

About four weeks after my father died, mysterious bills started arriving from local traders for items allegedly purchased by my father immediately prior to his death, including a substantial bill from a local hardware store. My mother and I searched high up and low down but could find no trace of the items that my father was supposed to have bought. There was never any question of my mother not paying these bills. While it was unlikely that there would ever be any debt collectors calling to the door, the insidious threat from these traders was far worse – the threat that they would 'put the word out'! These traders knew that our family valued our reputation for honesty and integrity above all else and they cruelly took advantage. Whatever small savings my mother had were soon gone.

We had two pigs that needed to be fed, so I was sent on a mission to find suitable scraps. The local vegetable shop had just received a trailer load of potatoes. The shop-owner was sorting through them, casting the sub-standard potatoes into a large bin in the corner. I asked if I could take these for the pigs. 'Of course you can young gosoon, help yourself'. I was delighted. At the end of the month my mother received a large bill for 'seed potatoes'. This time it was explicitly written on the bill 'Provided you pay within four weeks I won't put the word out'.

A short time later the local Garda knocked loudly on the door. He reprimanded my mother about ragworts growing around the perimeter of our property. My mother protested that she was not able to manage it and that I was doing whatever work I could when I got home from school. He told her that she had two weeks to get it cleared or she would receive a fine. Once again, our good name had to be protected. So that was it, my school days were over.

As the harsh snow of early 1954 descended, we had a small supply of coal left in the shed. If it were used sparingly, it would see us through this cold spell. But I noticed that our supply was dwindling faster than it should be. Surely nobody could steal our coal? One night I decided to sprinkle the shed floor with lime-dust, in order to solve this mystery.

The following morning the evidence was there for all to see. The white footsteps came out of the shed, out the gate, across the road and into the garden of our 'kindly neighbour', a neighbour who had offered to help and support us through our bereavement. My mother did not have the heart for confrontation, so we suffered the loss – and the cold!

Towards the end of the cold spell, we managed to heat the house with some stray ash branches that had fallen from trees nearby. As we sat in front of our makeshift fire, I could see the worried look in my mother's eyes. She had not paid the undertaker and we were now flat broke. How could she face him and tell him that we could not pay what we owed? Would we now lose our one last precious possession – our good name?

When the snow cleared, my mother decided that it was now time to face the music. She got up early in the morning, got dressed in her Sunday best and made the journey into the small town to see the undertaker. As she left the house, her face bore the expression of one of Ireland's martyrs, about to face the firing squad.

My mother explained our circumstances to the undertaker and promised faithfully to pay him as soon as we had the money. The undertaker just reached out and took my mother's hand and whispered gently, 'Don't worry missus, pay me whatever you can, whenever you can'. This simple act of kindness changed everything. Once again there were tears in my mother's eyes, but this time they were tears of hope. Maybe we would survive this after all.

And indeed we did.

Someone's Sons

Proinséas de Paor

The tiny village of Slade is at the end of the road; nobody passes through on their way to anywhere else, so the only people who get to see and enjoy its rugged beauty are those who make a positive decision to go there. It is tucked away in the south east corner of Ireland, on a rocky stretch of the Co Wexford coastline where the Hook Tower, Europe's oldest working lighthouse, stands guard at the entrance to Waterford Harbour. From the top of the tower you can see the village of Crooke, on the opposite river bank, and it is said that it was here, in 1120, Strongbow declared he would take Waterford, 'by Hook or by Crooke'.

Today, many people who want to escape the rush of city life are discovering the secret of its beauty and tranquillity, but in the early part of the last century things were very different. Visitors were virtually unheard of, and life for most of the inhabitants was a daily routine of work and sleep with very little time, or money, for leisure activities.

Except Sundays of course. Sundays were for going to church and gathering in groups around the castle to share the gossip.

Peter was a typical villager. He was born in Slade and by the outbreak of the First World War he had lived and worked there for over half a century. His home was a little thatched cottage on the dockside, he owned a small fishing boat, and he rented some land from Lord Ely's estate – one acre, three roods and thirty perches to be exact.

Peter's day consisted of fishing in the morning and working on the land in the afternoon. His prime aim was to provide enough food for his family – whatever was left over would be sold to pay for some of the other necessities of life. Life was not easy for Peter and his wife, Mary, struggling to provide for their children, but life was never easy for anyone in those days.

Peter's first wife had died and the children of that marriage were now grown up sufficiently to fend for themselves: John had joined the merchant navy, Tommy and Polly had moved to Cardiff in search of work, and Annie worked for a family in Wexford. There were still four young ones, however, that needed feeding and clothing, so the never-ending circle of work and sleep continued while the 'war to end all wars' was fought on foreign shores. Slade was a long way from the battlefields of Belgium and France, and the war was a long way from the minds of Peter and his neighbours. Until one morning in September 1916, that is.

Peter had left the dock early in the morning to catch the tide, the sea was choppy but not too rough, and there was a fair wind to fill the sails of his boat. With him that morning was his fourteen-year-old son, Patrick, who had left school that year and was now expected to contribute to the household. The lobster pots they had put out the previous day were a couple of miles or so offshore and he was hoping for a good catch. He needed the money the lobsters would provide; Mary had told him she wanted to make her annual trip to New Ross to buy shoes for the children in preparation for the winter – the rest of the clothes she would make herself, sewing and knitting during the long dark nights.

Peter knew these waters as well as any man alive and had chosen his fishing ground well, getting 21 lobsters from their fifteen pots. After re-setting the pots, he headed for home, with his mind already on the work to be done that afternoon, while Patrick fished for mackerel on the way.

Suddenly he was jolted out of his thoughts by a disturbance in the water no more than a hundred yards away. It was like nothing he had ever seen before; the sea was erupting in front of his eyes. Then his surprise turned to fear. He had never seen one before, but he did not need anyone to tell him that what was emerging from the sea was a German submarine. The bow rose high in the water and then, as it smashed down and levelled out, causing a wave that rocked the boat, he could see a machinegun on the deck and could clearly make out the number, UB17, on the tower amidships.

The submarine looked huge; it must have been eighty or ninety feet long and, even at that distance, towered high over the little sailing boat. Peter knew about a submarine sinking the *Lusitania* just ten miles off the coast of Cork the previous year, and now, as he attempted to reassure young Patrick, a hundred thoughts raced through his mind, 'What do they want?' 'What will I do?' 'I can't escape, they could shoot me out of the water'. He knew that even a glancing blow from the mighty metal monster would smash his little boat like matchwood, and send it to join his lobster pots at the bottom of the sea.

The sound of banging metal came from the submarine as a small group of uniformed figures appeared on the tower. They signalled him to move closer. There was really no choice but to do as they indicated, so he dropped the sail and edged closer, using the oars. He could hear them shouting, 'Haben Sie bitte etwas zu essen?' He could hear them, but he had no idea what they were saying. 'Hast du Fische?' Then a few words of English, 'Please, some food, have you fish, please help.'

A rope was thrown to their little boat and – still nervous, still fearful of what might happen – they tied up alongside. In broken English an officer explained that they had been at sea longer than expected and had run out of food. There were fourteen men on board and they had not eaten a proper meal for days. Without hesitation, Peter told Patrick to pass over the box of mackerel. 'Danke, Sie sind ein guter Mann.' 'Thank you, you are a good man. Please take this, we have nothing else to give you.' Peter and Patrick looked at the jar and wondered what it was; they had never seen Piccalilli before.

As father and son edged their boat away from the submarine, they could see sailors cleaning the fish as a small kerosene stove was set up on deck to cook them. With the Germans waving and calling out to them, they headed straight for Slade, catching just enough mackerel for dinner on the way. Patrick jumped from the boat, onto the dock, and ran as fast as his legs would carry him to show his mother the strange jar of Piccalilli.

'How could you do that?' Mary asked Peter when she heard the story, '… don't you know there's a war, they're our enemies.'

Peter's answer was a simple one, that showed his compassion. 'Mary, I couldn't leave them hungry; after all, they're someone's sons.'

RUSTY AND THE T-REX

Collette Cassidy Leonard

Alittle girl called Eve is peeping at her calendar. She loves October because that's when her birthday is, but most of all she looks forward to Halloween, and that's in October too. Eve really loves Halloween, but she has a problem.

Last year her dog, Rusty, was very nervous, he did not like the loud noises the fireworks made in the sky. October is his least favourite month.

One day in August Eve had a good idea. 'Rusty, we're going to celebrate Halloween today!' Eve thought it was a clever idea because there would not be any fireworks in August. 'Rusty, when the real Halloween comes in October you won't feel so nervous because you will have enjoyed one Halloween, in August,' she said.

Eve needed a pumpkin, but there are no pumpkins in August, so she decided to use her Mammy's peppers. It's a good thing her Mammy had three peppers, because the first two turned out a bit wobbly. 'Rusty, look how nice this pretend pumpkin looks!' said Eve. 'Hmm, not bad at all,' thought Rusty.

Eve looked out the window at the late August sunshine. It was time to go trick-or-treating. 'You can just go as yourself, a Wheaten Terrier. I'll brush your hair and we can pretend your beard is magic,' said Eve. She decided to wear her dinosaur costume and off they went trick-or-treating. It was not a success because people were not expecting a T-Rex and a dog with a magic beard on their doorstep in August.

Eve was still hopeful she could give Rusty a fun Halloween to remember. Then she said, 'Rusty we didn't get any treats but I will set up my bakery. It shall be called Halloween Buns.' Rusty waited on his mat for hours as Eve prepared all sorts of things. She had just learned how to make cinnamon rolls. Eve said, 'Perhaps cinnamon rolls are a bit too Christmassy for Halloween in August?' But she made them anyway.

Eve had one egg left, so she whipped up a side order of French toast with a spider design on top. Some of it got caught in his magic beard. 'Rusty, isn't it funny that we are both Irish but we can eat French toast? Maybe in France someone is eating Irish toast!', she said. Rusty just wished the Halloween Buns Bakery would stay open all year round.

The weather became cooler and the leaves started falling off the trees. Rusty knew Halloween was coming and it was October, his least favourite month. He was starting to feel anxious about the fireworks that would soon start. When the spooky night arrived Rusty felt his tail go down. That was a sign he was not feeling too good.

He decided to hide under the kitchen table, his own little kingdom where he felt safe. Eve, who loves Halloween, really did not want Rusty to feel scared. As he sat under the kitchen table, he noticed a T-Rex tail and the T-Rex passed him something that smelled like summer, something he remembered from the Halloween Buns Bakery. It was French toast.

Rusty thought about the lovely day in August and the smell of the cinnamon rolls that were a bit too Christmassy. He thought about his magic beard and the pretend pumpkin peppers. But most of all he thought about how loved he felt that day.

The T-Rex looked under the table. It was Eve. 'Rusty you ate all your French toast!' she said. Rusty's tail did a happy dance. He tilted his head up towards her for a pet. He then fell asleep and had a lovely dream.

He had not heard the fireworks. He had not even felt nervous.

'Goodnight my little Halloween Bun,' said Eve as she smiled to herself. Her plan had worked. Rusty was never afraid of Halloween again.

And he always looked forward to the reopening of Halloween Buns Bakery, in August.

(Based on a true story about my daughter Eve and her beloved rescue dog, a wheaten terrier named Rusty.)

No Space, No Place for Him

Jennifer Horgan and Simon Lewis

Based on contributions from parents of children with additional needs in Ireland 2021

They say it in a million different ways
but the message is the same.
There's no space, no place for him here.
The principal's office
drops a thousand decibels
And we're sunk,
plug pulled
hook slung.
I run my two gloved hands over the rail
like my boy would have done.
Pull another school-gate closed behind me,
numb, my list from the SENO shortening.

Exhausted, past performing.
Another place he can't go.
I'm open-boned, cold, struggling with my coat
whole years of being told *no*,
rejected by worn out phrases:
We can't make exceptions
It's more than we can give
We've a duty to tell you like it is
The department's left us no choice
Your child will never fit in.

There's no space, no place for him there
I tell my husband when I come home and he stares out the window,
mutters '… a few more to go, I suppose'.
His voice catching in his throat because he knows the ones left
on the list are more than twenty miles from where we live.
Our child will end up in taxis and buses with other kids like him.
He squeezes my hands tightly in his, kisses them,
goes upstairs to tuck him in. Later, I'll do it again.
My back, shoulders, limbs, ache from preventing his escapes,
bruises up my thighs where I've held him in the cage of my arms at
    night.
Hours of noise and fear inside of him, catching up on him. No end
    in sight for him.
My baby cries out for me to help, but where do I begin?
I'm done in by years of waiting, on appointments, assessments,
pre-screens, referrals, provisional diagnoses,
on CAMHs, on interventions, educational psychologists, speech
    and language therapists, on the DSE, the HSE, the DES,
the Acts never enacted,
All the state's paper trail, a littering to cover itself,
All the scraps, add up, come back, to little else.

There's no space, no place for him
He's one of thousands
In a waiting room nobody ever checks
Full of people like us
Wrecked from looking for placements in places left to rot
Schools let down, left short
Sent token emails, support in bullet points about nutrition.
Politicians making promises,
Forgotten, once they're in.
There's no space, no place for him,
But silence makes that decision
People don't know how much they could do for him
By asking why there isn't a support room in their school for him
By asking for help for someone other than themselves
By asking why boards of management care more about league tables
Or why schools are left banging on doors for basic reforms,
For real supports for our children.

There's no space for him, no place for him
Because maybe this is war
It makes it easier to understand if that's where we are
On different sides like spies taking notes, dug deep in our trench
At least then it makes sense. If you're my enemy,
If my child is a threat.

There's no space, no place for him
But what if our sides met?
If we helped each other out, didn't let our politicians rest
Forced them to build a system that puts every child first
Would we all not be stronger?
Could all of us, in our hundreds, rise up like a hot air balloon,
Together, one army, one platoon,
above the bombs blasting, the cuts, and the cracks
Couldn't we get something precious back?

JENNIFER HORGAN AND SIMON LEWIS

I miss my boy's laugh.

I want him to run through my door at the end of his day
Smile at what he's done at school, in his own time, his own way
I'd like to not put out fires nobody else can see
I'd like the fire to be in the belly of that balloon, fuelling us all up
   up up
into a dream.
And when all our kids grow up, they'll look around and see
anyone left on the ground.
who needs a hand, a different plan, who needs time outs,
quiet rooms or just a smile, a nod.
That's all we really want.
That's what life should be for him.
That's the world we should all want to live in.
Where no child is invisible
*Where there's never **no space, no place for them**.*

A FATHER'S LOVE

Alan Morrissey

Icount my blessings every day. 'Why?', you might ask. Because I am blessed to be father to two wonderful, beautiful girls, Rose and Grace – five years old, and eighteen months old respectively.

All of us, when we are fortunate enough to become parents, imagine what our children will be like as they grow up and make their way in the world. No amount of imagination, however, can prepare any of us for how our child, or children, will turn out; what they will look like, what they will do, what their personality will be like, what kind of temperament they will have, etc.

I am no different; in the lead up to the birth of Rose, I felt, at times, like no amount of preparatory work – which included reading numerous articles on parenting, attending antenatal classes and so on – could really get me ready for what lay ahead, whatever that might be. I was right.

When our baby arrives, it is the most amazing, magical day of our life. We are faced with this incredible, beautiful little person that we have helped to create, someone who we instantly love more than life itself, and we want to do our very best by them. When I recall how nervous and unsure I was whenever I did something for my daughter for the first time, I'm sure I wasn't alone. Changing her nappy, making her a bottle, whatever the task, we all question ourselves as to whether we are doing it right.

As she moved through the early stages of her life, from baby, to infant, to toddler, and then on to become the wonderful little girl she now is, I felt as though I was gradually becoming more confident as a father, and yet there are still times, even now, when I question whether I have done the right thing. Have I admonished her too harshly for being bold? Should I have just sat down to play with her for a while when she asked, instead of continuing to do chores or prepare the dinner?

When we go on to have more children we relax a little in the – mistaken – belief that we have learned enough raising our first child that will allow us to use the experience for the little ones that follow. However, and I shouldn't really be too surprised in saying this, every child is unique, and not all our experience is easily transferable. My Grace is no different in that regard, so there are still times when I feel as though everything I do with her, and for her, is being done for the very first time.

One of the regular features on the radio show I present is a parental advice slot for which we are fortunate enough to have the services of an excellent clinical child psychologist. Her sage advice is welcomed by the mothers and fathers of Co Clare, including me, especially when she covers a particular topic or gives specific advice. At that moment I become a listener as well as a presenter, and need her words of wisdom every bit as much as anybody in the audience at home!

Ultimately, though, I have come to realise that being a parent is a continual learning process. The journey, the quest for knowledge – whatever you want to call it – is an evolving story. No parent ever really knows all there is to know about the *right way* to raise a child. The right way for one child is not necessarily the right way for another, so we all just do our best and hope we'll get things right more often than we get them wrong.

As anyone lucky enough to have children will know only too well, becoming a parent can affect us in profound ways. One of the many ways in which it has affected, or changed, me is the extent to which tragic news involving children gets to me. Before becoming a father, I would read, or hear, a story about a child who was missing or who had tragically died, and it would, of course, make me feel very sad. Since becoming a father, though, I really struggle whenever I hear any news of that nature. My first thoughts are of my own two girls and I instantly become very emotional at the possibility – remote as it may be – of them ever being the subjects of similarly terrible news.

I have even found myself in this position while presenting my radio show. One of the most desperately sad and moving interviews I ever conducted, in a decade and a half of working in broadcasting, was during the first half of 2022. It was with a couple who, on Christmas Eve 2012, had lost their eight-month-old son to sudden infant death syndrome and were appearing on the show to promote a fundraising event for charity. One which they had organised in their son's memory. As they recalled their happy memories of his all too short life, and recounted the details of that awful day almost ten years earlier, I could feel myself becoming extremely emotional. I began to well up and had to muster all of my strength to finish the interview.

I'm sure I was not alone and have no doubt that all those listening at home were affected by the couple's story every bit as much as I was. However, I am also sure that, again like me, the listeners had nothing but complete and utter admiration for the couple. Not only for the way they somehow found the inner strength to carry on after their son's passing, but the way in which they channelled their energies, and their grief, into organising, in his memory, this fundraiser that would make a huge difference to a very worthy cause. To ultimately be able to create something so positive from such an unspeakable tragedy …

I'm lost for words, and still don't know how they managed it, but I have absolutely nothing but the utmost respect for them for doing so.

Speaking with parents who have suffered the devastating loss of a child has made me realise that getting the chance to be a parent at all, to be on that journey, to be afforded the opportunity to learn every day how to be a better father or mother, is an extremely precious gift that should be embraced and savoured.

It's a gift we should never take for granted, and one that I never do – every time I see Rose and Grace, every time I hug them, or hear them say 'I love you' is a timely reminder of just how very, very lucky I am.

FROM CORK TO NEW YORK

Treasa Goodwin-Smyth

How do you go from being a camogie player in Cobh, to a farm manager, to a nurse, and end up in the media? It takes a bit of doing and there are lots of ups and downs along the way, but it can be done – I know, because I did it.

Born in Cobh, I was one of ten children, and spent my formative years on the family farm, attending the local schools where I quickly developed a love for sports, especially camogie. You know what they say, 'take up sport and it keeps you on the right road in life'.

I was making something of a name for myself on the playing fields around Cobh, and there were those who said I had the skills to become a great Camogie player. Local success led to being selected to play with Imokilly county divisional team in Cork, but my reign there was short. I was fortunate enough to receive a scholarship to Gurteen Agricultural College in Tipperary, and from there I went on to start a career in farm management and accounting.

After a while I wanted to broaden my horizons and see a bit more of what the world had to offer so in the mid-eighties I emigrated to New York. I went to college to earn my degree as a NY state registered professional nurse, paying for my tuition by working as a nurse's aide at night. During those hectic years, I worked in many different areas of nursing and enjoyed every minute. My favourite areas were labour and delivery, and the operating room.

New York was exciting, but like so many immigrants at that time, I missed home, and decided that one way to overcome this would be to get back into camogie. The New York Young Ireland's Camogie Club was a great way to meet many Irish and Irish-American women and I had the honour of lining out with them for a number of years, winning a number of North American senior championships and later became PRO and spent twelve years as president.

In 2008 when Cumann Camogaíochta na nGael celebrated its 100th anniversary, I was selected by the US Camogie Association to travel to Ireland as liaison with the US team. In 2019 I returned to camogie, but this time as coach for the NY based Shannon Gaels where I enjoy sharing my knowledge and game skills with the younger players.

During Covid it was back to the books resulting in me becoming a nurse transformation coach whilst working as a nurse administrator for Warner Media. Over 30 years earlier, in conjunction with the New York GAA, I was the first ever woman to be involved in the broadcast of the Senior All-Ireland Hurling and Football Finals.

I am proud to be a member of many Irish organisations, to serve on the board of the Board of Celtic Irish American Academy and Project Children NY, and to have been the recipient of a number of awards from the Irish American community, including Cork woman of the year, and Grand Marshal of the Rockaway St Patrick's Day parade in 2003.

In 2008, my husband, Tommy, was chosen as Grand Marshal for the Fifth Avenue St Patrick's Day parade whilst I was in the WNBC TV commentary booth. For the 2022 parade, we were both behind the microphones, describing the event for Irish Americans all over the country.

We also keep them up to date with music and news from Ireland on *Ireland Calls*, which is heard worldwide on WVOX.com, and Spotify.

Sport remains high on my agenda and I have now completed numerous marathons in places including Scotland and Ireland, and get great pleasure in coaching others – most of whom are middle-aged and have never run before.

For all that life has given me, however, my proudest moments were the birth of my children Anthony and Lisa, and more recently, my grandchildren, Brendan and Sloane.

How do you go from being a camogie player in Cobh, to a farm manager, to a nurse, and end up in the media? Or, how do you go from where you are now, to where you want to be? You decide what you want and then take chances and work hard to achieve it. But the miracle isn't that we achieve our dreams, the miracle is that we have the courage to start.

A Divine Light

Sudhansh Verma

I was carried there by autogenic helicopter, surrounded by alien security, but I did not know where we were headed, so I was excited. It reminded me of my childhood in India when my father gave permission for me to tour a new school just because the principal wanted me there. But let me go back to where it all began.

It was strange. The journey continued for what felt like days as if the helicopter was fuelled by air, not petrol or diesel. No one spoke. It was as though the commander had ordered total silence until further notice. I wanted to get up from my seat to ask the commander where we were going, but I was locked in by my seatbelt. Outside all was dark. No moon or stars. And with no idea where we were heading, I had many questions in my mind.

Eventually the helicopter stopped. No one moved, but my seat belt opened and the arm rests folded back, as though I was supposed to rise. As I stood, some armed guards approached with big smiles, and fell in behind me as though I was the boss. I felt like a VIP. There was a strong wind blowing but everything seemed familiar, as though I had been there before.

The path was dark and upward, as we walked for a long time. I felt like a champion climber, but the heavily armed guards stayed close. I walked for miles, lifted by a loving wind that felt like a lover, giving me a sense of belonging but staying remote, like a one-sided romance. She played hide and seek with me, darting this way and that, like the elusive butterflies on my childhood farm, mesmerising me. It was a pure romance.

As happens in a dream, it seemed that I was both in the lead and at the back, chasing that romantic wind, stopping to allow it to catch up, so that I could hold her hand. I felt in love, but she remained out of reach, always moving away from me whichever way I went. She was there, embracing me, but not yet mine. I felt like a bee desperate for her pollen. As the saying goes, it is always the thirsty that goes to the well, and I was thirsty.

Like a child rejoicing in being alive, I was in love, I was exhilarated, happy, reaching out for the comfort of a loving partner, but I had no one to share my feelings with. I made a promise then, 'One day I will hold your hand and we will walk together.' I longed for your response but knew I still had to go on. As the poet said, I had promises to keep and miles to go before I sleep. And suddenly the image changed.

Shhh. There was a bullock cart waiting for me, complete with a bullock. I greeted him, but got no reply. He signalled for me to climb aboard. I jumped up as if I had a reserved seat there. Once again I said hello. I tried 'namaste'. No reply. I said 'hola', 'bonjour', 'salve', 'guten tag', 'marhabba', 'privet'. Nothing. I even tried Chinese. 'Ni hao.' Still no response.

The bullock cart continued in total silence, but I was glad to rest. The armed guards had gone and I was glad to have left behind the millions of steps I had taken in my adventure. I forgot about my loving wind and, somehow, I fell asleep.

*****

SUDHANSH VERMA

Awake and alert at last, my mind was filled with thoughts of the big event I was trying to organise in Dublin's Phoenix Park. It was to celebrate with my wife the Hindu festival of colours, Holi. It was certainly not easy to organise as it required permissions from the Office of Public Works (OPW) and the Gardaí.

It was a great show with the local community bringing home-cooked food and snacks which we all shared once we had completed the ritual, riotous exchange of colours. I was thrilled by the smiles on everyone's faces.

My wife, who is a foodie, liked the food even more than the people! At the end we were tired, covered in colours and well fed. Back in our apartment we had a wonderful sleep as if we had slept for ages. The beauty of this festival was the satisfaction it gave us.

Over the next few days life returned to normal and my wife took up charity work as I was not at home during the working week. We were learning to cope with the challenges of married life. I made mistakes but she forgave me and even overlooked them at times. I wondered what she expected of me but she just wanted to build a happy life together based on trust and love. If I had to judge this period, I would be lost as it just flew by so fast.

In 2004, our story made this headline in the *Irish Times*, 'They got married and fell in love.' Actually, I wanted to change it to say we 'grew in love'. Our marriage resulted from the deaths of two loved ones back in India.

It happened when I had gone back from Ireland to my home near Lucknow during my holidays, to look for a bride. My wife's parents and two of their friends were driving to meet my parents for the first time, with a view to arranging a marriage for one of their daughters. Along the way they were involved in a serious collision with a jeep. All four were unconscious.

A passer-by looked into the wrecked car and saw my father's phone number on a piece of paper on the dashboard. He called the number and my father answered. The call was a great shock as we had all been eagerly awaiting their visit. We immediately left for Lakhimpur District

Hospital where the injured four had been taken by ambulance. There we learned that only two would survive the accident. The owner of the jeep had run away and has still not been found. We focused on saving the lives of the two survivors.

My brother and I arranged for an ambulance to take them to a better hospital in Lucknow and we all set off, accompanied by Dr Himashu. Meanwhile, the family of the injured had been informed. There were three daughters, only one of whom was married. They rushed from Lucknow to see their parents and met up with our ambulance. I did not have the courage to face them and tell them how their parents were. With shaking voice Dr Himanshu told them to hurry to Lakhimpur Hospital and they left in tears. I will never forget that moment.

The next time I saw Surabhi (now my wife) was when she came to see her parents at the hospital on her scooter. But the first time I visited her at home I was in torn jeans and refused to eat any sweets. That made everyone suspect I was diabetic, and therefore possibly unsuitable. Then in came a Pink Girl. I have no words to describe the pureness of her beauty. I was sold.

What could I say to handle the scene. I was speechless. Instead, I tried to focus attention on the medical attention her parents needed to survive. I arranged to spend a couple of nights at the hospital to show my commitment and prove I was worthy of their 'pink' daughter. Not only that, I even agreed to ride to the hospital on the back of her scooter, although in that community a man was supposed to be the driver, and especially so as I was still a stranger to her. It also gave the impression that I did not know how to drive a scooter.

Days passed and the understanding between us grew, as her parents recovered fast. They were released from hospital and slowly dealt with the loss of their two family friends. Meanwhile the pink girl was becoming impressed by my selfless service and suggested an engagement before my return to Ireland, if that was acceptable to my parents. We completed the engagement but realised that in order to bring her to Ireland, we would have to be married. So, we arranged a small legal ceremony, just with the family, in the presence of the solicitor, Mr V.P., who signed the papers. A few days later I returned to my Karma Land, Ireland, as a legally married man. But this was not enough. I would still have to do a big fat Indian wedding where everyone is invited.

Some weeks later a date was fixed for the big wedding and I flew back to India. The wedding rituals were held at an auspicious place called Shantikunj Haridwar. A far from ordinary place, it is the domain of my spiritual guru, Vedmurti Tapnishta Pandit Shriram Sharma Acharya, who wrote 3,400 books and was a living god with 140 million followers. He was born as a pragya (wisdom) avatar to create thought revolution.

This is why he was important to me and to our marriage. In the gradual evolution of human development over the millennia, only rarely have multi-faceted geniuses with superhuman attributes appeared to elevate human consciousness. The Saint-Scholar-Philosopher Pandit Shriram Sharma Acharya undoubtedly belongs to this small, rare group. Born on 20 September 1911 in the village of Anwalkheda in Agra District, India, Acharya's whole life was devoted to clearing the way for the emergence of a new era of universal peace, harmony and goodwill.

Acharya followed a great Himalayan Yogi. He took part in the non-violent struggle for India's independence as a volunteer, went to jail a number of times as part of the freedom struggle, and worked for social and moral upliftment through spiritual means with the blessing of Mahatma Gandhi.

A social reformer, Acharya lived a simple, disciplined life of devout austerity. His writings explore solutions to the innumerable problems of today. He died on 2 June 1990. But his teachings live on in the influence they have had on people like me.

Surabhi and I got married after the blessings and two days later held a grand reception attended by four thousand people, including the entire population of my village.

As if that were not enough, a few days later my in-laws held their own reception. I had no more time as the holidays were over, so I flew back to Ireland alone, while Surabhi finalised her visa application. She eventually joined me in Ireland on an historic date: 11 September 2004.

There was more to come. We were informed that the apartment we were living in was about to be sold, and we had to vacate it. We were lucky to find another place nearby in Terenure. But days later I developed blisters on my face. The doctor diagnosed chicken pox! Apparently, it's rare in adults, so I had to isolate myself and rely on calamine lotion to ease the itching. Back in India, I would have had some alternative therapies, including a herbal healer and, of course, prayers.

Perhaps there's a message in that. During my period of isolation I reflected on my earlier vivid dream and the loving wind that remained just beyond my reach. It seemed to me that I found the answer to that dream in Surabhi, the wife who came to me through dramatic circumstances and shared in the playful mayhem of Holi in Dublin's Phoenix Park Gardens.

PATRICK

Brendan Power

It was still dark when he climbed out of bed, but that was normal for February, especially in bad weather, and weather didn't get much worse than it was on that Friday morning. It would be another hour or so before the sun crept in from the east and started to push back the night. With the wind rattling the windows of their small, completely exposed, cliff top cottage at the appropriately named 'Windy Gap', there was nothing to suggest that today would be any different to yesterday, or the day before. Nothing to indicate that in less than twelve hours, Patrick would enter the annals of history and be hailed as a hero, and nothing to suggest that he would never again return to his bed.

He moved quietly as he pulled on his clothes and left the bedroom to light the little paraffin oil lamp in the living area; he didn't want to wake his wife yet. As Margaret Keating she had been his childhood sweetheart, and now, sixteen years after becoming Mrs Cullen, she was mother to his nine children, and still the love of his life.

With the howling wind finding every little gap in the door and window frames, and the cold seeming to permeate through the stone walls, his first task, after braving the elements to reach the rudimentary outside toilet, was to light the fire before the rest of the family rose from their slumbers. In the inglenook fireplace, which dominated the little room, was a pile of driftwood that had been collected by Mikie and Jack, the two eldest boys, and this was soon ablaze, gradually forcing the cold to retreat.

It wasn't long before Margaret joined him and immediately started preparing potato cakes and a big pot of porridge to make sure everyone began the day with a full stomach. As the children began to emerge from the two small sleeping areas in the loft space, fifteen-year-old Nellie took over the cooking duties while her mother took care of two-year-old Cathy and three-year-old Bridie. There wasn't room for them all to eat at once so, with the youngest first to the table, the older ones warmed themselves with a cup of tea. There would be no school today as it was considered too dangerous to walk the mile or so to get there in the storm force winds.

Not everything came to a stop, however, and Patrick took Mikie with him down to the big burrow where, on the grassland behind the sand dunes, he had set snares the previous evening. The rain soaked them through, but the dunes provided some shelter from the worst of the wind as they made their way from snare to snare, eventually leaving with three rabbits that would afford the family a hearty meal that evening.

He had no work that day. For the last few weeks it had been too rough to launch his fishing boat, and the poor weather meant there was no casual work available on the local farms, but he was an industrious man and never allowed himself to be idle. After returning home with the rabbits, and whilst Margaret prepared them for the pot, he went to the shed to finish off a couple of lobster pots, ready for the season which would get underway in a few weeks' time. While he was there, he checked on another project he had recently completed. Underneath a piece of canvas sailcloth was a small bike he had rescued from a barn and fixed up; painting the frame to cover the rust, mending the punctured tyres and soaking the chain in oil to get it moving again. It would be a present for his youngest son, Patsy, whose seventh birthday was the following weekend. It was a present the young boy would keep for many years, even after he had grown out of it.

In the afternoon, Patrick used a break in the rain to go outside and see what he could do to block the gaps in the door frame. With the tide approaching its lowest ebb, the children used the opportunity to go down to the beach below the cottage and collect more driftwood. It was always plentiful during a storm. At around three o'clock they all heard a loud bang, and saw a flare in the sky; and they all knew what it meant. Someone was in trouble on the sea and the lifeboat crew was being called to action.

As soon as he heard it, Patrick grabbed his coat from the bedroom and said a hurried goodbye to Margaret and the children before mounting his bicycle, little knowing they would never see each other again. He was 40 now and had been a member of the Fethard on Sea's lifeboat crew for almost fifteen years. Rowing a 35-foot boat was heavy work and he wasn't sure how much longer he would be able to it, but for now those thoughts were put to one side; there was somebody out there in need of his help, and he would do whatever he could.

His ungainly old Triumph was kept in the little shed, where he made sure it was well maintained with the tyres always pumped up and moving parts regularly oiled. The heavy steel frame and the one and a half inch wide tyres were designed to cope with the poor roads, the steel chain guard and mudguards kept the dirt and rain at bay, and the spring-loaded carrier doubled up as a seat for the children. The foul weather meant there were very few people out on the roads that day but just after leaving home he met his young friend Martin Foley and only had time for a quick, and final, 'Hello' as he continued his ride in the wind and rain.

When he arrived at the boathouse, the *Helen Blake* lifeboat was on its trailer with two horses already being hitched up to tow it a few hundred yards to the dock where it would be launched. Most of the crew were already there and the rest were not far behind him.

At half past three, the boat was in the water and the rescue was underway. A Norwegian schooner, *Mexico*, had run aground on rocks surrounding the Keeragh Islands, about three miles offshore, and they needed to get the crew off the boat before it broke up.

At Innyard Point, a hundred yards or so from the dock, there is a semi submerged row of rocks that juts out into the sea and on board the *Helen Blake* the first task for the crew was to make sure they were well clear of them. There was no time to settle in. They had to be co-ordinated as soon as the shore crew cast off, and then row in unison straight out from the beach with the boat being rolled around by the incoming waves, before they could turn into the wind to face them head on. There were ten oarsmen and each man knew what was needed as they worked together like the well-drilled team they were, with Patrick occupying a position towards the stern where he could set the pace for the others to follow.

After clearing both the beach and the dock a shudder went through the entire crew as they recognised the enormity of the task in front of them. With strong winds and huge waves thundering in on their starboard bow, there was no way they could row a boat weighing almost four tons against an incoming tide; to do so would have needed a superhuman effort and would have sapped every last ounce of energy before they even reached the wreck.

Aware of this, coxswain Christy Bird made the decision to ship the oars and raise the sails, which would conserve energy as well as enabling them to cover the three miles between the mainland and the islands in a much faster time. It was no easy ride, however, tacking into the wind and being thrown around by the enormous seas. The two men in the bow took the brunt of it, having to turn away from the crashing water every time they hit a wave head on.

Perhaps they had a premonition, but hardly a word was spoken that fateful afternoon as the entire Cullen family stood outside their front door overlooking Fethard Bay, watching as the lifeboat pulled away from the shore, heading for the Keeraghs on its errand of mercy. As on previous occasions, the children were competing with each other to catch a glimpse of *Daddy*, but, sadly, none of them did.

Approaching the islands, they could see the stricken schooner held fast by the rocks in the midst of towering seas. As the waves, racing in from the Atlantic and across the Celtic Sea, hit the shallow water around the rocks, the energy normally used to drive them forward escaped vertically, increased their height and made them unpredictable. The cox knew the only way to effect a rescue would be to get between the ship and the shore so he formulated a plan he hoped would allow them to get the crew safely off. His intention was to steer to windward and come around the wreck on their port side.

The plan was working. The lifeboat was within a few yards of the ship and they were ready to take the crew on board. Suddenly, appearing to come out of nowhere, a massive wave swamped the boat, causing it to flounder in the rough seas. The men braced themselves as an attempt was made to get her away from the wreck, which towered over them, but without success.

Incredibly, a second, even bigger, wave poured over them, closely followed by a third, tossing the boat around in the direction of the island. Only a couple of hours after low tide, a vicious array of sharp rocks was hiding just below the surface, waiting for their next victim having already ripped gaping holes in the steel hull of a ship that dwarfed the tiny lifeboat.

As soon as they felt the impact and heard the sickening sound of splintering timber, the crew knew the boat was doomed. Everything seemed protracted. It was as though they were seeing things in slow motion, as they were thrown violently from their seats.

There was no way of them knowing it, and no time to think about it, but for Patrick, and eight of the others, the shattered boat was the last thing they would ever see before their life was extinguished.

It would be two months before Patrick's remains were discovered by a local man, walking his dog on a beach. One of his feet was missing and it is believed that after being thrown into the sea he was trapped by some of the wreckage, remaining there until his foot broke away at the ankle allowing the body to free itself and be carried ashore by the tide. His body was placed in a coffin and taken home in a cortege fit for a hero.

Patrick's final resting place is beneath a small stone cross in the grave-yard surrounding Poulfur church, a mile from Fethard on Sea, where his name – and those of his thirteen comrades – is engraved on a monument as a lasting reminder of the selfless bravery displayed on that fateful day in February 1914.

'Ar dheis Dé go raibh a n-anamacha.'

Our Authors

ADI ROCHE is the founder and CEO of Chernobyl Children International (CCI), focusing on the relief of suffering experienced by children as a result of the 1986 Chernobyl nuclear disaster. Under her leadership, CCI has provided over €105 million for the areas most affected by the disaster and has enabled over 25,500 children from the areas to come to Ireland for vital medical treatment and recuperation.

AIDEE LYONS was born in Killester Park, Dublin, second youngest of nine children. She is a part-time civil servant, is married to Des, and has two energetic dogs, Shadow and Daisy, who she describes as their life-savers, taking them on regular walks near their North Dublin home. They are proud parents of two daughters and proud grandparents to two grandsons.

ÁINE TONER is Features Editor for the *Belfast Telegraph* and *Sunday Life*. She spent most of her career so far in Dublin, editing national magazines and is Ireland AM's book reviewer. She is the author of two books, *Let's Talk About Six* and *The Four of Us* and can be found on Twitter: @aineltoner.

ALAN CORCORAN is a broadcaster with South East Radio in Wexford, presenting the *Morning Mix* programme, prior to which he worked for RTÉ Radio 1 and RTÉ 2FM. He has also presented TV programmes on

TG4, and presented two country music series on RTÉ TV. He is a current affairs presenter dealing with local, national and international issues.

ALAN MORRISSEY is a native of Dublin who has lived in the Limerick/ Clare area for more than 25 years. Alan has worked within the radio industry for fourteen years and is the presenter of *Morning Focus* on Clare FM, which is broadcast every weekday morning from nine o'clock until midday. He has also spent time working in the communications industry.

AMY MOLLOY currently works as Public Affairs Correspondent with Mediahuis Ireland, covering investigations and consumer issues. In 2018, she was awarded *Young Journalist of the Year* and *Upcoming Business Journalist of the Year*. Amy hails from Wexford and holds a bachelor's degree in law, and a masters in journalism.

ANNA CLASSON is the Head of Region for the Royal National Lifeboat Institution (RNLI) in Ireland. From Rosbeg in Co Donegal, she has recently been appointed as the RNLI Trustee to the Board of the International Maritime Rescue Federation and is a former member of the Board of the Charity Regulatory Authority. Anna is the RNLI delegated member of the National Search and Rescue Committee in Ireland. Her family includes her husband, Ross, a fisherman, four sons and her four grandchildren.

ANTONIA HENDRON is Managing Director of M50 Truck & Van Centre, M50 GSE and M50 Power Solutions, headquartered in Dublin, and in 2022 was elected as President of the Society of the Irish Motor Industry. She is the chairperson of the Vehicle Testing Network and was a finalist in the EY Entrepreneur of the year in 2020.

BERNADETTE O'SULLIVAN returned to her native county in 2018 following a long absence, swapping the city streets of Dublin for the country fields of Kerry and, the sight of a nearby shopping centre for a distant view of the Macgillycuddy Reeks. She continues to work in the public service, has become a trial-and-error gardener and is the proud mother of three teenage boys.

BRID STACK is a former senior ladies' footballer who, over a twelve-year period, was part of the Cork team that won eleven All-Ireland titles, nine Munster titles and ten National League titles. She also won seven All-Star awards, was named Munster Player of the Year in 2012 and overall Ladies Football Player of the Year in 2016. Most significantly, the team was awarded RTÉ Team of the Year by public vote in 2014. She joined the Greater Western Sydney Giants women's Australian Rules team in 2020.

CAROL DOOLEY has presented on local, national and international radio stations for many years, including BBC Radio 1, Classic FM UK/Europe, Jazz FM London, Radio City in Liverpool, Classic Rock 2.9 KISM WA USA, and more. She has been Programme Director for a number of stations in Ireland and the USA, and currently presents the daily *More Music Drive* show on Sunshine 106.8, as well as *KCLR Classics* on KCLR, and weekend shows for Nation Radio UK. She also teaches Bikram Yoga!

CATHY KELLY is a former journalist, and now an author who, since 1997, has written a string of bestselling novels, which have been translated into many languages and have reached number one in Ireland, the UK and Australia. She is also passionate about her work as a UNICEF Ireland ambassador. Cathy lives in Wicklow and has twin sons, Murray and Dylan.

CLIFTON WROTTESLEY is an Irish Olympian who represented Ireland in the 2002 Winer Olympics and was Chef de Mission in 2022. Born in Dublin, he was brought up in Galway, Spain and London, and educated at Eton College, Edinburgh University and Royal Military Academy Sandhurst before joining the Grenadier Guards. He is the 6th Baron Wrottesley, 14th Baronet.

COLLETTE CASSIDY LEONARD is an artist who lives in Sallins, Co Kildare. She has two young daughters and two dogs: an Irish terrier called Amber and a rescue Wheaten terrier called Rusty. She loves to sketch the charming relationship between her daughters and their much loved four-legged family members, and posts daily sketches on Instagram at one_sketch_per_day.

DAMIEN BALLOUT was born in the UK and moved to Ireland in 2007. He met his wife Emma in 2011 whilst working in financial services. They have two boys together, Henry and George. Damien is passionate about cooking and loves nothing more than the kitchen being full of people, sampling his culinary delights.

DAMIEN TIERNAN is Double Gold IMRO winning radio presenter of *Deise Today,* in Waterford. He was South East Correspondent for RTÉ for over two decades and wrote two bestselling books, *Souls of the Sea* and *The Ecstasy and the Agony,* which was shortlisted for Sports Book of the Year. He has also produced and presented a number of documentaries, both on radio and television, and guest presented *Nationwide* a number of times. He lives in Waterford and is father to two brilliant teenagers.

DAVID CARROLL lives in retirement in Dublin. He is passionate about Ireland's maritime heritage and has contributed many articles to the *Waterford Harbour Tides and Tales* online blog. In 2020, he wrote a history of the Dunmore East RNLI entitled *Dauntless Courage* – a celebration of the lifeboats, their crews and the maritime heritage of Dunmore East.

DES KENNY was born in Galway on 15 March 1950. He attended Scoil Fhursa, Coláiste Iognáid and University College Galway from which he graduated with a BA. He was then offered a Master's Course in the University of Sorbonne where he graduated with a Matrise es Lettres. He returned to Galway in 1971 and began working in the family bookshop.

DES KIELY is a professional graphic designer living in Wexford. He has traced his family history back to the village of Stradbally, Co Waterford, and the house where his great-great-great-grandfather, John Kiely, a fisherman, was born in 1778. Apart from writing books on Wexford local history, his hobbies include photography, music and art.

EIMEAR NI BHRAONÁIN is a journalist from Carlow town. She is a former regional correspondent for the *Irish Independent,* and author of

Is Féidir Linn: A Golden Ticket to Moneygall – a souvenir book on the visit of Barack Obama to his ancestral Irish home. These days she presents *KCLR Live*, the flagship show for KCLR, from 10.00 a.m. to 12.00 p.m.

FRAN CURRY spent almost twenty years as a professional musician and record producer, with some of Ireland's finest artists before moving to radio in 1996 where he has worked in music presentation, current affairs and arts presentation as well as many years in radio management. He currently presents the IMRO Award winning Tipp FM daily flagship show *Tipp Today*, and hosts a weekly music show on the SKY platform.

HELEN COLLINS is a Skibbereen based solicitor, collaborative practitioner, mediator and author of *A Short Guide to Divorce Law in Ireland*. As the grandniece of General Michael Collins, she delivers the family address at the annual commemorative service at Béal na Bláth. A former chairperson of West Cork Arts Centre and current chair of West Cork Food Festival, she is mother to three children and is unstinting in her promotion of all things West Cork.

JACK GOWER, whose grandmother grew up in Skibbereen, is a professional ski racer who won the world junior giant slalom title when he was just sixteen. He represented Ireland in the Alpine Combined (Downhill and Slalom) at the Beijing Winter Olympics where he recorded Ireland's best ever alpine skiing result.

JAMES SAUNDERS is a teenage student at Tullamore College. An accident in April 2019 resulted in a traumatic brain injury which he continually fights to overcome. He is planning to write more in the future about his life experiences in the hope that it may help others in a similar position.

JASON SMYTH competed, undefeated, in international Paralympic events for eighteen years, winning 21 gold medals in the 100 and 200 metres. Recognised as the fastest Paralympian on the planet and one of Ireland's most successful athletes, he retired in 2023 to take up a role as strategy manager with Paralympics Ireland. He was born in Derry and spent a few years in the USA and London before settling in the Belfast area with his wife, Elise, and two daughters, Evie and Lottie.

JENNIFER HORGAN is the author of non-fiction book *'O Captain, My Captain': one teacher's call for change in the Irish education system*. She writes for the *Irish Examiner* as their education columnist and has had creative work published in various print and online journals.

JOE DUFFY is one of Ireland's most popular broadcasters, presenting *Liveline* five days a week on RTÉ Radio 1. Born in Dublin, he studied at Trinity College, and now lives in Clontarf with his wife, June, and their triplets, Ellen, Ronan and Seán.

JOHANNE POWELL was born in Norway. She met Alan in 1975 when they were both working on the oil tanker *Berge Septimus*, and they married two years later. After sailing together for a further six years they settled down in Fethard on Sea, Co Wexford where their daughter, Siobhán, was born in 1984. Together they were her loving full-time carers for over 36 years before they lost her in 2020.

JOHN DORMAN was born in Sligo and now lives in Dublin where he works as an architect. Much of his spare time is spent sketching and recording the changing face of Dublin. He is also a human rights advocate with a special focus on Palestinian solidarity activism.

JOHN FULHAM is a native of Limerick City. He was a Bank Manager with AIB for 24 years before moving to the Irish Wheelchair Association. He has competed in four Paralympic Games, World Championships, was European Champion over 100 and 200 metres in 2003 and has won three Dublin Marathons. He is married to Mary, and has a six-year-old son, Harry. His hobbies include reading, cinema and Munster Rugby.

JOHN MAGNIER is one of Ireland's most successful businessmen. and a former senator in Seanad Éireann. Amongst his many business interests, he was a major shareholder in Manchester United, and is recognised as Ireland's leading thoroughbred stud owner based in Fethard, Co Tipperary. Married to Susan, the couple have five children.

JP McMAHON is a chef, restaurateur and author. He is co-owner and culinary director of Michelin-starred Aniar Restaurant and award-winning Spanish restaurant Cava Bodega in Galway, and also runs the Aniar Boutique Cookery School. In 2022 JP launched JP McMahon Culinary Consultancy and works nationally and internationally. He is the founder and symposium director of Food on the Edge, the annual international food symposium.

KATE DURRANT is a regular contributor to *A Word in Edgeways*, on RTÉ Radio 1, and *Pause for Thought* on BBC Radio 2. The editor of two regional newspapers, her work has been published by the *Irish Examiner* and the *Sunday Independent*, commissioned by *The Holly Bough* and *Loft Books*, shortlisted in the 2021 *Hammond House International* literary prize, and printed in several anthologies.

LYNDA BRYANS is a broadcaster and public speaker based in Northern Ireland. For three decades she was news anchor, reporter and presenter across local and national TV including BBC and ITV networks. She is now Course Director of Broadcast Journalism at Belfast Metropolitan College. She is married to Mike Nesbitt and has two grown up sons.

MARIA BRICK was shortlisted for the Write by the Sea Flash Fiction Award 2022, the Colm Tóibín International Short Story Award 2019/20/22, the Anthony Cronin International Poetry Award 2020 and was Crime Story winner in *Woman's Way* 2019. She has featured on RTÉ's *Sunday Miscellany* and Radio Kerry's Inspirational thoughts/ Poetry and spoken word events. Maria lives in Killorglin, County Kerry with husband Ger and precious daughter Tam.

MARY CATHERINE MURRAY trained as a human rights lawyer. She is fascinated with international relations and involved in the needs of vulnerable people. Her time in Israel described in her story was her first trip abroad. She hopes to return one day to visit the all-natural spa, and although she likes to cook, she is still learning how to prepare a good picnic!

Archbishop MICHAEL JACKSON is the Church of Ireland Archbishop of Dublin. Born in Lurgan, Co Armagh, he was educated in Trinity College, Dublin; St John's College, Cambridge; The Church of Ireland Theological College, Dublin; and Christ Church, Oxford. He was ordained in 1987 and elected Archbishop of Dublin in 2011. He plays an active role in the wider Anglican Communion, especially in the areas of ecumenism and inter-faith dialogue.

MÍCHEÁL Ó SCANNÁIL is a journalist for RTÉ. Having previously reported for the *Irish Independent* and having presented RTÉ's flagship news programme for children, *news2day*, he is currently working as a radio reporter for *Morning Ireland* on RTÉ Radio 1 and as a TV presenter for special programming events like the St Patrick's Day Parade.

MIKE NESBITT began his career as a sports reporter before switching to news, covering many major moments of the Troubles and peace process. After setting up the Commission for Victims, he was elected to the Northern Ireland Assembly where he is currently serving his fourth term. He is married to Lynda Bryans and has two adult sons.

NEIL BANNON has been in the commercial property business for over twenty years, and is acknowledged as Ireland's leading retail property expert. Neil has led shopping centre projects from site assembly through design to opening through successive rent reviews and unit re-lettings, has led asset management teams and dealt with both the acquisition and disposal of large-scale shopping centres.

NIALL O'DOWD emigrated to the US in 1979 from Thurles, Co Tipperary and is the founder of *Irish America Magazine*, IrishCentral. com, and the *Irish Voice* newspaper. He received the Irish President's Distinguished Services Award and an honorary doctorate from University College Dublin for his work in helping undocumented Irish in the US, and winning President Clinton's support for the Irish Peace Process.

NICOLA TALLANT is a Dublin-based award-winning journalist, author and podcaster. Specialising in covering organised crime, she regularly appears on TV and radio, and is executive producer of a number of crime documentaries and the award-winning podcast *The Witness in His Own Words*, based on her bestselling book *The Witness*. She hosts her own weekly show: *Nicola Tallant's Crime World*.

OLIVER SEARS is a London-born, Dublin-based art dealer and gallery owner, son of a Holocaust survivor and founder of Holocaust Awareness Ireland. A former trustee of Holocaust Education Trust Ireland, he is a frequent contributor to radio and newspapers including RTÉ and the *Irish Times*. He tells his family story *The Objects of Love* through a collection of precious objects, documents and photographs that survived the war and describe individual lives under Nazi occupation. Oliver has lived in Ireland for over 30 years.

ORLAITH FRAWLEY is from Coolfore in Co Meath. After operations to remove two brain tumours as a young girl, she now lives with Von Hipple-Lindau syndrome, requiring annual MRI scans.

PHILLIP KHAN-PANNI is a retired professional speaker and trainer, Fellow and co-Founder of the Professional Speaking Association, and author of thirteen books, mostly on communications skills. Formerly senior copywriter at Reader's Digest, his career highs have included starting a direct marketing agency, MD of a magazine publisher and Express Newspapers' most successful ever classified ad manager. He now lives with his wife, Evelyn, in Naas where he writes CVs for senior people, and is active in Toastmasters International.

PROINSÉAS DE PAOR lives in County Wexford and remembers as a child being told the story of the German submarine by his aunt, Sister Gabrielle de Ste Victoire, of the Little Sisters of the Poor.

DR RICHARD TERRES is a geophysicist who, along with his Wicklow-born wife Christine, has worked and lived around the world; from the jungles of Sumatra and Papua New Guinea to the deserts of Oman and Jordan. They are now flirting with retirement and have settled on the Hook peninsula in Wexford to be close to the sea. They have one daughter, Katie, who lives in London.

ROBERT ALDERSON studied at the Royal Northern College of Music before joining Scottish Opera for three years. He then gained his Dip Ed Mus in Secondary Education and took up a position as Head of Music in a large comprehensive school in Lancashire. Since then his teaching career has taken him across the world and he has been a vocal tutor, guest lecturer and has given masterclasses in many countries including Ireland. In 2003 he joined the full-time teaching staff as a Principal Vocal Lecturer at the TU Dublin Conservatoire.

LT General SEÁN CLANCY joined the Defence Forces as a cadet in 1984, and has spent a considerable period of his career as a Search and Rescue pilot. He was the commander of the crew who received the Marine Medal for Meritorious Service in 2002. He has served in a number of appointments including two years as a non-permanent member of SHIRBRIG, the UN standby Brigade, and a year with the European Union Force in Bosnia as the military advisor to the Force Commander.

SIMON LEWIS has published two collections of poetry, *Jewtown* (2016) and *Ah, Men!* (2019). *Jewtown* was a finalist in the Shine/Strong Award in 2017. In 2015 he was the winner of the Hennessey Prize for emerging Poetry, and runner-up in the Patrick Kavanagh Prize. He is a primary school principal in Carlow Educate Together.

DR SINÉAD McCOOLE is a historian, curator and author of several books and plays, who has worked in the area of Irish culture, arts and public history for almost three decades. She is curator of the Mna100. ie website on behalf of the Department of Tourism, Culture, Arts, Gaeltacht, Sports and the Media, an online resource relating to the role of women, 1921–1923, which is the final part of the government of Ireland's Decade of Centenaries Programme.

STEPHEN BREEN is Crime Editor with the *Irish Sun*, having previously worked as Crime Correspondent with *Sunday Life* in Northern Ireland. Author of one book and co-author of another two on organised crime, he was also Newsbrand's Crime Journalist of the Year in

2018, a previous Sunday Journalist of the Year in Northern Ireland, and received a Certificate of Merit at the Justice Media Awards in 2022 for his work in highlighting trauma experienced by victims. He is also a regular contributor to RTÉ *Prime Time* and national radio stations.

SUDHANSH VERMA was born in India, and educated in India, the UK and Ireland, where he has lived since 2001. Aside from his business interests, he is, amongst other things, a Hindu priest, a peace ambassador, co-founder of the first Hindu temple in Ireland, founder of a charity school in India and a member of the Dublin Interfaith Forum. He is married to Surhabi and they have two daughters, Shivali and Savi. His next project is to plant 30,000 oak trees in Ireland, one for each Indian living and working here.

TOM FATHOM is from Killucan in County Westmeath but has lived in Newcastle Co Wicklow for almost 30 years. Married to Audrey with one daughter, Lorna, who is a primary school teacher. His hobbies are amateur dramatics, growing vegetables and walking his dog on the beach. He took early retirement in 2019 and has now enjoys movie extra work.

TOMMY FLEMING has been described as a singer 'whose voice has the remarkable ability of taking you into his world'. Unique, honest, emotive, powerful, dynamic and an instrument of passion are some of the terms which have been used to describe his voice – a voice that has reached out through a myriad of genres, sometimes difficult to classify. There is no doubt that whether it is his arrangement of 'Danny Boy', 'Fiddlers Green' or 'Sweet Sixteen', Tommy delivers each song with a finesse that casts its magic over spellbound audiences.

TOMMY MARREN is a current affairs broadcaster with Midwest Radio in Co Mayo, and anchors the main chat show every Monday to Friday morning from 9.00 a.m. to 11.00 a.m. He is also a playwright and his works include *It's the Real McCoy*, *Nobody's Talking to Me* and *3 Hail Mary's* – all of which have successfully toured Ireland, England and the USA over the past ten years.

TONY GATELY is a recently retired electrician, living in Galway with his wife, Rita. They have four *wonderful* children. He has been an occasional contributor to *Ireland's Own*, and, as a guitar player and singer, has written some hymns which he has sung with his church choir.

TREASA GOODWIN-SMYTH was born in Cobh and attended Gurteen Agricultural College in Tipperary before moving to America where, with her husband, Tommy, she now presents *Ireland Calls*, the longest running Irish radio show in the USA.

WILL FAULKNER is the flagship broadcaster on Midlands 103 and has previously worked with Dublin's 98 FM and KCLR 96 FM. He is married to Alix and they live in Co Offaly with their two children. He has raised over €250,000 for local charities and is passionate about mental health awareness.